BUILDING SELF-ESTEEM
THROUGH THE
MUSEUM OF

25 Original Projects that Explore and Celebrate the Self

BY LINDA R. ZACK, M.ED.

EDITED BY PAMELA ESPELAND

Free Spirit
PUBLISHING

Library of Congress Cataloging-in-Publication Data
Building self-esteem through the museum of I : 25 original projects that explore and
    celebrate the self / by Linda R. Zack.
    p.   cm.
    Includes bibliographical references and index.
    ISBN 0-915793-92-X (pbk. : alk. paper)
      1. Self-esteem in children—Study and teaching (Elementary)—Activity programs.
    2. Self—Study and teaching (Elementary)—Activity programs. 3. Education,
    Elementary—Activity programs. I. Zack, Linda R., 1947–
    BF723.S3B85   1995
    370.11'4—dc20   95-19669
                                                                                CIP

Cover and book design by MacLean & Tuminelly
Illustrations by Nancy Tuminelly and Lisa Wagner
Index compiled by Eileen Quam and Theresa Wolner

10 9 8 7 6 5 4 3 2 1
Printed in the United States of America

The alternative projects ideas for creating slides (page 8) and filmstrips (page 9) are from *TNT Teaching: Over 200 Dynamite Ways to Make Your Classroom Come Alive* by Randy Moberg (Minneapolis: Free Spirit Publishing, 1994) and are used with permission of the publisher.

FREE SPIRIT PUBLISHING INC.
400 First Avenue North, Suite 616
Minneapolis, MN 55401-1730
(612) 338-2068

DEDICATION

With love, I dedicate this book to Jason and Tracey, my children, whose own "explorations of self" inspired me and taught me about individuality and the real meaning of life.

And to Sheppard Faber, my soulmate, whose love, belief in my ability, and daily encouragement helped me reach this goal. Without his support, this book would still be filed "creatively" in colored folders.

ACKNOWLEDGMENTS

I want to thank . . .

My parents, for constant nurturing; my son, Jason, for all the computer help; and my daughter, Tracey, for second opinions. A special thanks to the law firm of Faber & Gitlitz and Ed Raduns for letting me move into their offices during the summers.

Helene Gralnick, for lifelong friendship; Carol Springer Fishbein, for "nagging" me to finish; Bonnie Morgenstern, Rita Ginsburg, and my sisters, Diane and Norma, for much needed "breaks;" and Ellen Kempler-Rosen for expert advice. I also wish to acknowledge the inspiration I received from Bapuji and Gurudev.

An appreciation to Marilyn, a former colleague, whose special way of teaching showed me how to reach gifted adolescents and find my true niche in education.

Love and thanks to all of my gifted resource students at Arvida Middle School, who over the years have embraced my crazy ideas.

Pamela Espeland, a truly gifted editor, helped me to understand the importance of form. Her guidance was essential and always encouraging. Special thanks to Pamela, Judy Galbraith, and Liz Salzmann at Free Spirit for believing in me and my dream.

CONTENTS

LIST OF REPRODUCIBLE PAGES

INTRODUCTION

When you recall memories of your own school experience, chances are you think of your friends, favorite teachers, shared experiences, field trips— and all of those projects you had to do! You remember the projects that turned out great, the ones that fell apart, and especially the last-minute ones that took all night and drove everyone in your family crazy. Occasionally there was a school project that was unforgettable. You felt challenged, it was truly meaningful, and everyone else thought yours was terrific.

What if all students could feel that kind of success when given a school project assignment? The projects in *Building Self-Esteem through the Museum of I* offer your students that opportunity. This book is a collection of activities and ideas that invite students to turn inward, explore who they are, and express what they find by creating products that are exciting and unique because they represent themselves. Diversity becomes a celebration in the classroom as students share and evaluate each other's products.

The premise of this book is that you, the teacher, are a museum guide who arranges exhibits and tours. You provide the motivation, intro- duction, guidelines, and time and space for hands-on exploration. The projects are student- directed, and you are the facilitator, shifting learning from being teacher-centered to student- centered. The projects are open-ended, encouraging divergent, original thinking, yet they can easily be incorporated into competency-based curriculums.

Most of the activities are artistically connected, allowing for creative expression in a variety of media and forms. There is a wonderful inner dialogue that happens when a person creates art, and your students really come to know themselves better. As each project is an exhibit of the self, several projects together become a museum of the self, a museum where we come to learn, to marvel, to question, to open our minds and sharpen our sensibilities.

I originally developed and used these projects with gifted students in grades 6–9 in order to meet simultaneous objectives involving creative thinking and affective needs in my classroom. My gifted students usually remain in my program for three consecutive years, so it has always been my personal challenge not to repeat projects. (I can't even repeat a joke with this group!) After years of creating my own curriculum and receiving compliments from colleagues (and students) about my creative teaching, I felt it was time to gather my projects together in a way that others might find useful. These projects have been classroom-tested for twelve years, so you can feel confident about intro- ducing them to your students.

You'll probably find, as I did, that the results for both you and your students include the joy of discovery and the excitement of learning beyond a traditional, more limiting curriculum. You'll be amazed, as I was, at the tears, laughter, and applause you'll witness, along with the self-esteem building and bonding your students will experience.

How to Use This Book

Building Self-Esteem through the Museum of I is ideal for enrichment classes, language arts, humanities, or visual arts programs. It is also suitable for counseling groups, youth groups, and home schooling. Most of the projects are long- range efforts that can be completed in or out of the classroom. All promote creativity as opposed to conformity.

The projects and themes provide a framework for units that can be adapted to almost any upper elementary or middle school/junior high class or special program; most can even be used in high school. You might view this book as a sourcebook of ideas for infusing affective education and sensitivity into any curriculum plan.

The book is organized in a manner that allows easy planning for teachers and group leaders. Each project includes learning objectives, a materials list, ideas for introducing the project, experience notes (glimpses into my classroom), ideas for expanding the project, suggestions for alternative projects, a list of resources, and a student handout. Role performance, related curriculum, and learning styles are indicated for each project so you can see them at a glance. The student handouts are written in a simple, conversational style and guide students through each step of the activity, from pre-planning to completion. All of the instructions students need to complete each project are included on the handout. Before beginning a project, you should thoroughly familiarize yourself with the handout.

I suggest that at the beginning of the school year, you select a handful of projects that appeal to you. Work them into and along with your regular curriculum. These projects are not meant to be the sole curriculum, and they will lose their impact if offered to students one after the other. Consider them as "dessert"—and yes, your students will ask for more!

The time you allot for each project will vary according to the ability levels and ages of your students and the configuration of your class. I have deliberately not assigned specific times because I don't want to limit you or your students in any way. However, you may find it helpful to know what happens in my classroom.

My classes are 47 minutes long, five days a week. Many of the projects take about two weeks to complete—longer if there are school interruptions, assemblies, field trips, vacations, etc. A few projects, such as "My Sculptural Self," "Cartoon Journal," and "Personal Recipes," require minimal amounts of time but can be broadened and expanded to take longer. As far as your own classroom goes, you'll simply need to decide how few or how many of the ideas and suggestions to use, and watch how quickly or slowly your students proceed through a project. As in any individualized program, some students will begin right away, with energy and enthusiasm, while others will procrastinate, exhibit confusion, and lack ideas. As the facilitator, you will want to ask for progress reports, work with each student individually when needed, and offer help and motivation. Set deadlines based on your experience with a particular group, but please keep in mind that flexibility is the key to success and enjoyment with these projects.

About the Resources

As noted above, each project includes a list of resources. *These are always meant as suggestions, not requirements.* Over the years, as I have used these projects with my students, I have collected books, postcards, slides, etc. that have worked well for me. I promise that you will find others that work equally well for you. Please don't be discouraged if you can't locate or obtain a specific resource listed for a particular project. Instead, use my suggestions to brainstorm your own ideas. Consider this a creative challenge for you, just as the projects are meant to be for your students.

If you can't find a book on an individual artist, look for more general books that include works by that artist (along with many others). Use the library resources available to you—in your school media center, your neighborhood or county library, a local college or university library. If you live near an art museum or art school, you'll find a wealth of possibilities there. In time, you'll compile your own lists (and files, and shelves) of resources for your favorite projects. I would be delighted if you chose to share some of your "finds" with me.

Preparing Your Room

Is space "the final frontier"? It certainly is in my classroom! I am fortunate to have a classroom that is actually a garage. My room seems like a museum at times because I find it difficult to throw anything away. Most objects are "project possibilities" to me, so I keep all sorts of things on open shelving or in plastic containers. We recycle and reuse everything! I have become a pack rat for plastic bottles and containers, corrugated cardboard (light bulb packaging makes wonderful Greek columns), colored foam and sponge, fabric scraps, plastic shoe trees, chopsticks, notions, clear molded plastic packaging, wood scraps, small jars, egg cartons, Styrofoam packing, etc. Students love to watch my enthusiasm when they bring in "stuff" and I tell them about the possibilities for redefinition and reuse.

My students are required to begin the year by bringing in a small bottle of white glue, a pack of colored markers, and two old magazines with pictures. These become community property and are stored collectively. It's essential to have the basics on hand: a supply of newspapers, masking tape, colored construction paper, scissors, hot glue guns and glue sticks, rulers, yardsticks, a paper cutter, paint (tempera and acrylic), and paint brushes. Other supplies can be brought in by students.

I distribute a "wish list" to parents and students in the fall which asks for a lot of junk. They laugh and clean their closets. Many parents begin hobbies only to abandon them, so we benefit if only we remember to ask. Most parents really do love to help. One can never have enough baby food jars, coffee cans, or ping-pong balls. Ask for laundry baskets and storage containers, too. My essential motto is: "If you don't ask, you don't get." Once my class received two dozen produce department aprons for paint cover-ups and many slightly damaged plastic baskets from a grocery store.

If you don't have a water source in your classroom, keep a supply of gallon water containers on hand and a few buckets to clean paintbrushes.

Works in progress may cause problems, so emphasize respect for projects and property. When students bring in supplies, insist that they keep them in large shopping bags marked with their names. Try to create a storage space for these.

I also like to keep a few completed projects on hand to inspire students and show examples of careful work and crafts skills. Be careful not to show too many examples of anything artistic, or you'll squelch creativity and inhibit risk-taking.

Evaluating the Projects

Teachers often find it difficult to evaluate student projects that are personal and artistic in nature. This is understandable. Self-esteem is closely tied into any project that involves a reflection of self, and we worry that our evaluations might shake or bruise a student's self-esteem. For this reason, I feel that evaluations must be linked to qualities one can measure objectively— neatness, completeness, crafts skills, commitment, cooperation, and effort. When evaluating projects from this book, you can measure a student's performance in those areas as well as the student's expression of ideas, language skills, oral presentation, and, of course, any content-related material in the cognitive domain.

Evaluations may be done via group or individual conferences (determined by the type of activity, group, or individual), oral presentations, visual displays, use of "criteria checklists," a point system, progress reports, journal writings, or individual notes written to students. Each project in this book includes suggestions for evaluation, some more detailed than others. I encourage you to be as creative with your evaluations as you want your students to be with their projects.

Documenting the Projects

Whenever possible, I recommend documenting the students' projects on film. This gives students a record of what they have done (and a way to see growth when compared to later projects) and exciting materials for their portfolios; it gives you a potential showcase of student projects. Slides work best, but the trend is to use video equipment if you have it available. Be sure to take good close-ups.

My students and I take still photos as well; they like the extra copies, and when they return years later to visit, it's easy to look at photo albums quickly. It's a great teaching moment when a former student reminisces with pride and enthusiasm about a past school project.

Sharing the Projects

At the end of each project (or group of projects), create your "museum." Try to arrange exhibit space in your classroom, as well as a display in the media center or a hallway showcase. Use clothesline displays, hang things from the ceiling, tape drawings to the walls, and clear off the desks for a week. It's very important for students to experience the final step in the creative process: peer approval.

Many students have anxiety about sharing their projects in oral presentations. Encourage them to relax and see this as an opportunity for growth in a safe, supportive environment. To be able to express your ideas is an essential skill, and these projects provide a wonderful showcase for that experience. Projects should always be shared with classmates.

Occasionally hold a "museum opening" during the day for other classes to visit—in your room, if appropriate, or in the media center. An evening exhibit could be arranged in the cafeteria, with formal invitations and refreshments. Students could act as museum guides, or "docents," walking their visitors through the various exhibits, giving brief talks and explanations. If you have musical students, ask them to perform, or invite school band members to participate. By all means, treat your students as creative artists, and they will live up to your expectations.

Let Me Know How These Projects Work for You

For me, the absolute payoff for these projects is the total absorption I see in my students as they work on them. They learn new skills, gain profound insights about who they are, and truly bond with classmates. As their teacher, I am constantly stimulated. No two projects are ever the same. I learn more about my students from their projects than I ever could in hours of forced conversation. When they work with their hands and express their feelings through art, there is an opening for real communication. Then the learning begins.

I invite you to create a museum in your classroom. I would welcome any comments on your experiences. (Photographs of your student's projects would also be very welcome.) Please let me know how these projects work for you. Write to me in care of Free Spirit Publishing, 400 First Avenue North, Suite 616, Minneapolis, MN 55401-1730. I hope to hear from you.

Linda Zack
Miami, Florida

THE PROJECTS

"YOU BELONG TO YOURSELF. YOU CAN ONLY BE A TOTAL HUMAN
BEING TO OTHERS WHEN YOU KNOW WHO YOU ARE."

Louise Nevelson

"IF WE LOOK AT OURSELVES EVERY DAY A LITTLE,
WE CAN EVENTUALLY SEE THE WHOLE PERSON."

Herbert Holt

Personal Slide Show

Picture flashing images on a screen in a darkened room, each one part of a visual poem that represents a particular student. For this project, each student will create a "photo essay" that is a self-portrait by virtue of the abstract or representational images he or she chooses to photograph.

Role Performance

Students produce a slide show about themselves.

Related Curriculum

Art, Music, Photography

Learning Objectives

By the end of this project, students will be able to:

* plan a "shoot"—a list of photos to be taken
* use a 35mm camera to take slide photos
* show creativity in choice of photographic similes, metaphors, and abstractions that reflect the self
* use a photo copy stand, if available
* produce an audiocassette of music selections to accompany the slide show
* create a title slide
* edit the slide show
* present the slide show to the class

Learning Styles

Affective, Individual

Materials Needed

* copies of the "Personal Slide Show—Starring Me" handout (pages 10–11) for each student
* 35mm camera(s)
* 35mm film for slides, enough so each student can take at least 36 photos (48 is best to allow room for editing)
* audiocassette recorder/player, blank audiocassettes
* slide projector with carousel tray
* screen
* photo copy stand (optional, but great for photographing small objects or pictures from books)

Doing the Project

1. Introduce the project by telling the students that they are going to create personal slide shows. Use questions like the following to begin a discussion, or have the students write responses in their journals.

   ▶ Can you think of some *nouns* that can be used to represent feelings or moods? What about "balloon" for "happy"? "Feather" for "giggly"? "Cat" for "cuddly"?

   ▶ If you wanted to show a "sad person" or a "happy person" in an abstract way—*without* showing the person—what colors or images would you choose?

   ▶ How could you show interesting things about yourself in an abstract way—your hobbies, talents, family, likes, dislikes, and so on?

   ▶ How could you "picture yourself" without actually taking pictures of yourself?

2. Distribute the "Personal Slide Show—Starring Me" handout. Read through it with the students. Answer questions and provide explanations and details as needed. While students are working on their slide shows, be available to offer advice and assistance at each step.

3. Schedule the student presentations. Reserve the necessary audio-visual equipment (slide projector with carousel, audiocassette player, screen).

4. Conduct oral evaluations of the slide shows. Seek student feedback.

▰ EXPERIENCE NOTES ▰

This is a very exciting project for students to produce and share with each other. It's wonderful to do early in the school year, as a way to help students get to know each other, or as a culminating project, when students have bonded and are willing to reveal more about themselves. It's suitable for all age and ability levels, as only the sophistication of the photos and/or music will change.

Expanding on the Project

▪ View and discuss some of the "time capsule" films that depict years of history. Often, television networks show these at year-end, just before the New Year's holiday. Check your district film library for possibilities.

▪ Explore and discuss published photographic essays.

Alternative Projects

▪ Have students prepare photo collages or flip books using still photos, following the same general guidelines as for the slide show (think abstractly, be creative).

▪ Have students create their own slides. Blank slides, available at professional camera supply stores, can be written on or drawn on with extra-fine, felt-tipped permanent markers.

- Have students create their own filmstrips. Blank filmstrips are available at camera stores for a nominal fee. Use fine-tipped markers to draw the images. Check a commercial filmstrip to find out the size of each frame (count the sprocket holes along the sides). Then draw lines to separate the frames. Otherwise the images might be too large or too small to project correctly.

- Have students create their "slide shows" on transparencies and show them on the overhead projector. Anything drawn or printed on regular paper can be copied onto a transparency.

Resources

Polaroid Education Program, 575 Technology Square–2, Cambridge, MA 02139. This program offers excellent classroom support. There is no membership fee, and you receive great classroom materials, discounts on film, and opportunities for free cameras. Write on school letterhead stationery to enroll.

Allard, William Albert. *The Photographic Essay.* (Toronto: Bulfinch Press of Little, Brown & Company, 1991.)

A Day in the Life . . . series. (San Francisco: Collins Publishers, a division of HarperCollins Publishers; several volumes available.) Large-scale photographic essays of countries around the world.

Evans, Art. *First Photos: How Kids Can Take Great Pictures.* (Redondo Beach, CA: Photo Data Research, 1993.)

Moberg, Randy. *TNT Teaching: Over 200 Dynamite Ways to Make Your Classroom Come Alive.* (Minneapolis: Free Spirit Publishing Inc., 1994.) See especially "Media Materials," pages 35–56.

Steichen, Edward. *The Family of Man.* (New York: Simon & Schuster Trade Division, 1987.) A classic.

Turner, Robyn Montana. *Dorothea Lange.* (Boston: Little, Brown & Company, 1994.) Dorothea Lange's photographic essays brought the reality of suffering migrant workers to the public's eye for the first time.

PERSONAL SLIDE SHOW

Starring Me

1 Brainstorm a list of things that make you one of a kind—a unique person in the world. You might include your . . .

characteristics

favorite things

favorite people

friends

family

beliefs   causes   talents

special places

. . .and anything else you can think of.

hobbies

2 Write your brainstormed list on a separate sheet of paper. Next to each item, describe one or more photographs that might represent it. Be creative, and think abstractly. *Examples:* If you're a track star, you might take a photograph of blurry running feet. Or you might picture a pair of old, worn-out running shoes. If fashion is your thing, show an unusual angle of a full closet. If you're a messy person, show your room. If you love the beach, show footprints in the sand, your shadow on the beach, or wet swimsuits and towels hanging up to dry.

PERSONAL SLIDE SHOW

3 Working from your brainstormed list and descriptions, plan a "shoot." Go take pictures! For special shots, take two or three to make sure to get the best one. Try different exposure settings, different angles, different lighting. (This is called "bracketing.")

4 Plan a title slide. Your title slide will introduce your slide show and list the credits (your name and the names of any people who helped you). Be creative! Come up with an unusual title, then think of an unusual way to show it. *Examples:* If you're a beach person, write your title and credits in wet sand, surround them with shells and seaweed, then photograph your composition. Or write your title and credits in colored chalk on a chalkboard or sidewalk. Or stick magnetic letters on a refrigerator, car, or locker. Or . . . ?

5 While you're waiting for your slides to be processed, select and record music to accompany your slide show. The music you choose should reflect your personal style. It should complement the images you will show. You should not need to write words to go along with your slide show. Your music and images should say it all.

6 When you get your slides, look through them very carefully. Evaluate each one. Does it say what you want it to say? Next, select the slides you want to include in your slide show. (You probably won't include all of the slides you took.) Then put your slides in the order you want to show them. (It might help if you listen to your music while you're organizing your slides.) Finally, number and label each slide.

7 Rehearse your slide show. Make any changes you feel will improve it. You will become very familiar with the images, but your viewers will only see them once. Be sure to allow enough time for each slide to really be seen.

8 Tell your teacher when your slide show is ready to present to the class.

My Sculptural Self

Help students build self-esteem by creating monuments to themselves. For this project, each student practices planning skills while imagining and sketching a sculpture representing him or her. The sculpture is all imaginary and does not have to be built, just planned. The possibilities are endless, and each choice along the way must be carefully considered, as it will reveal self-concepts. This project gives students an opportunity to explore the vocabulary of the sculpture form of art, which should be part of the learning experience in class discussion.

Role Performance

Students design and plan a sculptural monument to themselves.

Related Curriculum

Art, Humanities, Language Arts, Guidance

Learning Objectives

By the end of this project, students will be able to:

* make detailed plans
* think metaphorically
* communicate ideas in written form
* use appropriate vocabulary of the sculptural art form
* exhibit some understanding of the ideas and work of some well-known sculptors
* look inward and reveal ideas about the self

Learning Styles

Affective, Individual

Materials Needed

* copies of "My Sculptural Self: Feeling Monumental" (pages 15–16) and "Sculpture Proposal" (page 17) handouts for each student
* art books and/or slides of sculptures and sculptors
* white drawing paper
* drawing pencils

Doing the Project

1. If possible, begin this project with a visit to an art museum or sculpture garden. In any event, have plenty of films, filmstrips, slides, and books on sculpture available for students to explore.

2. Use some of the basic vocabulary of sculpture as much as possible to enhance the illusion of the student as sculptor/art connoisseur. Examples:

   form
   armature
   mass
   positive and negative space
   monumentality
   movement
   three-dimensional
   expressive
   open or closed space
   solid
   compact
   protruding forms
   kinetic

   Joshua Taylor's *Learning to Look: A Handbook for the Visual Arts* is an excellent reference to have on hand.

3. Distribute the "My Sculptural Self: Feeling Monumental" and "Sculpture Proposal" handouts. Read through "My Sculptural Self" with the students. Answer questions and provide explanations and details as needed. While students are working on their slide shows, be available to offer advice and assistance at each step.

4. When all of the sculptural portraits and proposals are complete, allow time for students to share them with classmates, asking for positive feedback. Display the portraits around the classroom, or arrange to display them somewhere else—perhaps the art room.

5. Evaluate the projects, or have students evaluate each other's projects. You might assign each student to review one project and suggest that the evaluations take the form of newspaper articles ("New Sculpture Proposed for City Park"). Ask the students to consider questions like these when writing their articles:

   ▶ What will the sculpture add to its surroundings?

   ▶ Is it something that many people will enjoy?

   ▶ Will it be a tourist attraction?

   ▶ What will be the most interesting thing about the sculpture? The most appealing? The most surprising?

EXPERIENCE NOTES

Expect discussions to include values regarding the cost of public art, materials costs vs. time and creative input, abstraction, and the meaning of art in general.

Expanding on the Project

▪ Invite a local sculptor to visit your class during this project.

▪ If your community has outdoor public sculptures, find out who commissioned them and invite someone involved in the process to speak to your class. If a sculpture exists, most likely there will be documentation about the origins of the work and a bureaucrat who is knowledgeable. Begin your search for public art with a query to the city commissioners. You may end up taking a field trip or hosting a slide presentation in your classroom.

▪ If there is a college or university in your area, invite someone from the Art History Department or Humanities Department to speak to your class. Request that they bring slides to show.

▪ Check your school's film catalog for biographies of major artists, or rent videos about artists.

▪ A good follow-up activity would be for students to plan a sculpture of someone else—perhaps a teacher, close friend, relative, or public figure. In discussion, explore whether it is easier—or more difficult—to make the kinds of decisions necessary for this type of project. Can objectivity be taken for granted?

- Encourage research and discussion about the universal problem of the effects of pollution and vandalism on valuable and historic public art. Brainstorm solutions.

Alternative Projects

- Have the students create a display of "Mr. and Mrs. Potato Heads," using real potatoes. Have each student decide whose face to portray—their own, someone else's, or a fictional fantasy face. Encourage the use of other fruits and vegetables, too.

- Have the students photograph objects or parts of objects, then trim the photos to eliminate all background, reducing each element to its simplest form. These fragment photos can then be glued together in three-dimensional constructions. Have toothpicks or wooden Popsicle sticks on hand for use as hidden armatures.

Resources

Students will love studying the sculptural works of Claes Oldenburg, George Segal, Red Grooms, Marisol, Picasso, Henry Moore, Louise Nevelson, and Niki de Saint Phalle, to name just a few. Visit your local library or school media center for books, slides, prints, postcards, posters, or whatever you can find on these and other important sculptors.

Educational slide sets (or individual slides) about sculpture can be purchased from most major museums. The best sources are:

- Hirshhorn Museum and Sculpture Garden, Smithsonian Institution, Independence Avenue at 8th Street, SW; Washington, DC 20560; telephone (202) 357-3091. Photography Department telephone (for ordering slides): (202) 357-3273.

- The Museum of Modern Art, 11 West 53rd Street, New York, NY 10019; telephone (212) 708-9400. Mail order department (for books, slides, and posters): (212) 708-9888.

For good background information on sculpture, try one or more of these books:

- McConnell, Gerald. *Assemblage: Three Dimensional Picture Making.* (New York: Madison Square Press, 1976.)

- Massey, Sue. *Learning to Look: A Complete Art History & Appreciation Program for Grades K–8.* (Upper Saddle River, NJ: Prentice Hall, 1991.)

- Paine, Roberta M. *Looking at Sculpture.* (New York: Lothrop, Lee and Shepard Co., 1968.)

- Taylor, Joshua. *Learning to Look: A Handbook for the Visual Arts,* 2nd edition. (Chicago: University of Chicago Press, 1981), pages 87–90. An excellent resource for beginning art students.

My Sculptural Self

Feeling Monumental

You are incredibly special! In fact, you are such a wonder that a sculpture of you must be created as soon as possible! Your job is to plan your sculpture. You will think about what you want it to show and create a drawing—a "sculptural portrait"—that includes and reveals your ideas in such a way that an artist could actually create a sculpture from it. You won't actually be making your sculpture. But someday, maybe someone will.

Your sculptural portrait must depict your very essence. It should reveal your unique attributes, character, and personality in some way. Much can be revealed in a sculptural portrait through choices made during the planning stages, and all of the choices are up to you. This is an exercise in planning and decision-making. Use visualization techniques to "build" the sculpture in your mind.

As you plan and create your drawing, consider the following questions. Jot down some answers on paper to guide you along the way.

1 Who will the artist be? Someone famous? An unknown artist? A friend? You? Be specific. Give reasons for your decision.

2 Who has commissioned the sculpture? Was it your idea, the artist's idea, or did a group make the decision? (What group?) Why would someone want a sculpture of you?

3 What *medium* will the artist use to create your sculpture? (In other words, what will it be made of? *Examples:* wood, clay, stone, cement, glass, vinyl, plastic, notebook paper, cardboard, Jell-O, mashed potatoes, erasers.) Or will it be made of *mixed media*—more than one material? Be specific.

My Sculptural Self

4 Will your sculpture have one or more colors? Describe the colors. Why did you choose these particular colors?

5 What will the style of your sculpture be? Modern? Traditional? Abstract? Outrageous? Why? How does this style relate to you?

6 What will the dimensions of your sculpture be? Specify the height, width, and length, since your sculpture will be three-dimensional. What about the weight? Can you guess how much your sculpture will weigh?

7 What pose will you strike for your sculpture? Will you be seated/ Standing? Lying down? Sitting on a horse? (This is called an *equestrian* pose.) Asleep? Standing on your head? Talking on the telephone? Pose can affect the dignity of your sculpture, so be certain about the image you want to portray.

8 Will your sculpture include any "props"? If so, describe them carefully and explain the symbolism involved with each. What purpose will a particular prop serve? What statement will it make? What will it say about you?

9 How much will your sculpture cost to make? Will more money be spent on the materials or on the artist's fee? Why?

10 Location matters. Even a great work of art can look terrible in an inappropriate place. What location will you choose for your sculpture? Where will it look best? Describe the location in detailed terms. Consider the weather, the temperature, the traffic (foot traffic, car traffic, train traffic, airplane traffic), and anything else you can think of. Will it be indoors or outdoors? Will it sit on the ground, on cement, on a marble floor, in water, on sand? Or will it hang from a ceiling or jut out from a wall?

11 Give your sculpture a creative or meaningful title. If you like, you can include your name, a quotation or poem that is meaningful to you, or anything else you think should be included in the title.

12 Now that you've planned your sculpture, summarize your plans on the "Sculpture Proposal" page. Then, using drawing paper and pencils, create and attach a carefully prepared and labeled sketch to your proposal. Add details, notes, arrows, and color where appropriate. Use whatever written communication is necessary to explain your plan.

Sculpture Proposal

Prepared by: _____

My Name

on: _____

Month, Date, Year

Artist's Name: _____

Commissioned By: _____

Medium or Media: _____

Color or Colors: _____

Style: _____

Dimensions: _____

| Height | Width | Length | Weight |

Pose: _____

Props: _____

Artist's fee: _____ Cost of materials: _____

TOTAL COST: _____

Location: _____

Title: _____

Attach your sculptural illustration to this proposal.

Cartoon Journal

We love reading cartoons and comics because we often see slices of our lives mirrored in humorous interpretations. What home or office doesn't have some meaningful clipped cartoon on a refrigerator or bulletin board? We laugh and say, "That's so true!" Even editorial cartoons help us smile in the face of hard times or disaster. Expression through "line" is fun and often very revealing.

Role Performance

Students draw cartoons.

Related Curriculum

Art, Language Arts, Social Studies

Learning Objectives

By the end of this project, students will be able to:

- find humor in everyday situations
- use and improve their elaboration skills
- complete a detailed cartoon drawing about some event or experience from their personal life

Learning Styles

Affective, Individual

Materials Needed

- copies of the "Cartoon Journal: Creating Life Lines" handout (pages 21–22) for each student
- examples of work by cartoon artists
- black, fine-line felt-tipped pens or markers, or very dark, sharp pencils
- white unlined paper

Doing the Project

1. A few days before introducing this project, ask students to bring in a cartoon from a magazine or newspaper, or have some examples of cartoons available in the classroom. Use the following prompts and questions to generate discussion:

   ▶ Have students share their cartoons orally. Which ones depict real-life situations or scenes?

   ▶ Ask why they chose those particular cartoons to bring to class.

   ▶ Point out the wide variety of drawing styles in the cartoons and have students identify differences. Which cartoons are more detailed? Which are simpler? Which have background drawings? Which use balloons to indicate dialogue or thoughts? What are the different lettering styles? Are some characters more realistic than others? Call attention to thick vs. thin lines, shading, three-dimensional effects, and anything else that seems interesting and worth noticing.

   ▶ Compare single-frame to multi-frame ("strip") cartoons. Which seems better for telling a story? Why? Discuss the advantages of each type of cartoon.

2. Introduce the work of cartoon artists Lynda Barry, Jules Feiffer, Gary Larson, Paul Palnik, Saul Steinberg, and Bill Watterson ("Calvin and Hobbes"). Include other artists you know about whose work you enjoy and appreciate. Invite students to tell about their favorite cartoonists and why they like them.

3. Distribute the "Cartoon Journal: Creating Life Lines" handout. Read through it with the students. Answer questions and provide explanations and details as needed. While students are working on their cartoons, be available to offer advice and assistance at each step. The students should make their own decisions about what and how to draw, but they may want or need to bounce ideas off of you.

4. When the students have finished their cartoons, allow time for sharing with classmates, asking for positive feedback. Display the cartoons around the classroom. If your school publishes a school newspaper, see if the editor will agree to include some of the cartoons in future issues.

EXPERIENCE NOTES

There are no mistakes or "bad" drawings in this project. Students should be loose and enjoy themselves. Some will get very involved in tiny, intricate drawings with many characters, while others may be content to create a simple scene. Whatever their style, the students will learn that all journals need not be "just words."

Expanding on the Project

▪ Turn this project into a long-term journaling activity by continuing it for several weeks or months. Have the students create one or two cartoons each week depicting incidents from their lives, their personal reactions to events in the news, etc. They might even create "characters" representing themselves, their families, and their friends.

▪ If students already keep more traditional written journals privately or for other school subjects, suggest that they begin to include cartoons as well as words. They can clip cartoons from newspapers or magazines or create their own. Or they can add sketches to their journals.

▪ When you assign a paper or a report, give students the option of putting it in cartoon form. For inspiration, have copies available of *The Cartoon History of the Universe* by Larry Gonick.

▪ Use this project to introduce an in-depth study of editorial cartoons and their impact on public opinion. Include historical figures (Daumier, Thomas Nast, etc.) and modern talent (Don Wright, Morin, etc.).

▪ For students who are very interested in cartooning, there are many excellent resources you can direct them to. Start with Scott McCloud's *Understanding Comics*.

Alternative Projects

■ Newspaper comic strips are an excellent way to teach students how to use quotation marks when writing stories. Save a large quantity of comics, enough to give each student one or two. Instruct the students to place quotation marks before and after the words in the balloons, explaining that these are what the characters are saying (or thinking). Next, have the students rewrite the comic strip stories in prose, describing the scenes, including the dialogue (in quotation marks), and adding pronouns, verbs, and transitions as necessary. They can staple the strips to their finished stories.

■ Have the students collect several week's worth of cartoons (editorial cartoons, comic strips, cartoons from magazines) and compile them in notebooks or hand-made booklets. Ask them to write one or two sentence descriptions of each cartoon, or to give a reason why they like a particular cartoon.

Resources

Your daily newspaper is a readily available source of many cartoons. (Don't forget to check the editorial pages.) Try to find copies of alternative newspapers as well, since they often publish more daring and less mainstream cartoonists.

Gonick, Larry. *The Cartoon History of the Universe.* (New York: Doubleday, 1990.) Follow up with Gonick's *The Cartoon History of the Universe II.* (New York: Doubleday, 1994.)

McCloud, Scott. *Understanding Comics: The Invisible Art.* (New York: HarperCollins, 1994). This giant comic book examines the art-form of comics, including the use of line, the vocabulary of comics, timeframes, color, history, styles, important cartoon artists, and much more.

Moberg, Randy. *TNT Teaching: Over 200 Dynamite Ways to Make Your Classroom Come Alive.* (Minneapolis: Free Spirit Publishing Inc., 1994.) See especially "A Basic Course in Cartooning," pages 57–85.

Palnik, Paul. *Eternaloons: The Palnik Anthology.* (Columbus, OH: Creative Light Press, 1991). For ordering information, write to: Paul Palnik, P.O. Box 09342, Columbus, OH 43209. Cartoon posters by Paul Palnik are available from Free Spirit Publishing. Call 1-800-735-7323.

CARTOON JOURNAL

Creating Life Lines

1 On a separate sheet of paper, brainstorm a list of situations, events, or experiences from your own life that might make interesting cartoons. Your list should include at least eight ideas. For inspiration, picture yourself in a variety of settings. Examples:

- You in the middle of your room
- You in the school cafeteria
- You at a shopping mall
- You at a family gathering or holiday celebration
- You during a difficult time (hurricane, accident, funeral, exams, courtroom, etc.)
- You baby-sitting, doing chores, helping a neighbor
- You at the beach, summer camp, grocery store, neighborhood park

The possibilities are endless!

Cartoon Journal

2 Select a situation, event, or experience from your list to turn into a cartoon. Then create your cartoon, using pens, fine-line markers, or sharp pencils. Keep these guidelines in mind:

- Your cartoon can be humorous, or it can be serious. Not all cartoons are funny. In fact, some of the greatest cartoons have been *very* serious.

- Include activity, variety, and commentary (a title, dialogue, thoughts, etc.).

- Add interesting details that help to tell your story or explain your situation, event, or experience.

- Don't worry about whether or not you are a "good drawer." (Many successful cartoonists believe that they don't draw very well. But they bring a unique style and perspective to their work that communicates their message.) You can use circles and sticks to represent people.

- Play with point of view. Will you "see" the characters in your cartoon from close up or far away? (Will they be big or little?) What if you took a "bird's-eye" view and saw them from above?

- You might try drawing your cartoon in the style of a cartoonist whose work you appreciate and enjoy. Study examples or books. Can you imitate his or her characters, lettering, and details?

MY THEME PARK

Who could put a value on the price of a ticket to a theme park dedicated to one of your students? This activity allows students to imagine, plan, and create models of their very own "Busch Gardens" or "Disneyland" which totally honors them. Students will be using found objects, would-be trash, and recycled materials for much of this project.

Role Performance

Students design theme parks.

Related Curriculum

Language Arts, Math, Graphics, Art

Learning Objectives

By the end of this project, students will be able to:

- create and follow a plan
- explore flexible use of materials
- use creative thinking skills
- exhibit crafts skills and attention to detail
- explain ideas to their peers in an oral presentation

Learning Styles

Cognitive, Affective, Individual

Materials Needed

- copies of the "My Theme Park: A Great Place to Visit" handout (pages 26–27) for each student
- brochures from theme parks
- graph paper
- large sheets of drawing paper or newsprint
- pencils, rulers, tape measures, scissors
- pieces of plywood, thick cardboard, foam core, or other material to use as bases—any size up to 16" x 20"
- tape, glue, hot glue guns, glue sticks, and other adhesives
- found or recycled materials supplied by the students—whatever they want to use

Doing the Project

1. Create a bulletin board display of theme park brochures. Then initiate a discussion that focuses on theme parks in general. Ask questions like these:

   ▶ Why do people go to theme parks?

   ▶ What are they looking for?

   ▶ What are some characteristics all theme parks have in common?

   ▶ What are some of the attractions all or most theme parks offer?

   The discussion will be guided by the amount of personal experience your students have had with theme parks. If you live in California or Florida, this may be considerable, and explanatory discussion may not be necessary.

2. Distribute the "My Theme Park: A Great Place to Visit" handout. Read through it with the students. Answer questions and provide explanations and details as needed. While students are working on their theme parks, be available to offer advice and assistance at each step.

3. The evaluation process should include an oral presentation in which each student explains his or her project to the class. You might set up a "Theme Park Expo" for display in the classroom or a communal area of the school. The theme parks are also excellent for Parents' Night displays or school open houses. If your community hosts a city or county Youth Fair, your students' theme parks would make great entries.

EXPERIENCE NOTES

Set some general guidelines for scale in advance. A maximum height of 15" is reasonable, with a maximum base of about 16" x 20".

Allow several weeks for students to work on their theme parks, especially if your time is limited to one class period per day (or less). They will need time to think about and plan their projects, search for and gather materials, play with designs, and construct their scale models (a sometimes challenging process).

Expanding on the Project

▪ If possible, plan a field trip to a theme park in your area. You might schedule this as an introduction to the project. Students can use part of their time to gather information and take notes that may help them in designing their own theme parks. Bring along a camera and snap pictures of attractions, refreshment stands, park maps, and other special features to post on the bulletin board. (Of course, you might also schedule this as a wrap-up to the project—a way to reward students for completing their theme parks.)

▪ Invite an architect to visit your classroom and bring models or slides of various types of projects (homes, office buildings, shopping malls—and, if you're lucky, theme parks). Or see if a local college or university has an architecture department. Students there might be willing to share their knowledge and show their work.

▪ Invite someone from a local hobby shop to visit your classroom and demonstrate model-building.

▪ Have the students select music that would be appropriate for their theme parks. They can record their selections on audiocassette and include the recordings in their displays or class presentations.

Alternative Projects

- Use theme parks as a subject for problem-solving. Have students list the positive and negative aspects of theme parks, then brainstorm possible solutions to the negative aspects.

- Instead of creating theme parks, students might use the same procedure and skills to design towns, countries, or even planets that celebrate them.

Resources

Write to chambers of commerce, visitors and conventions bureaus, and state tourism offices and request brochures about theme parks to use as samples. According to the U.S. Travel Data Center, these are the Top Ten theme parks in the United States:

- Walt Disney World (Buena Vista, Florida)
- Disneyland (Anaheim, California)
- Universal City Studios Tour (Universal City, California)
- Knott's Berry Farm (Buena Park, California)
- Six Flags/Great Adventure (Jackson, New Jersey)
- Busch Gardens (Tampa, Florida)
- Sea World (Orlando, Florida)
- Cedar Point (Sandusky, Ohio)
- Kings Island (Cincinnati, Ohio)

Throgmorton, Todd. *Roller Coasters of America.* (Osceola, WI: Motorbooks International Publishers & Wholesalers, Inc., 1994.) A fascinating history of the roller coaster—plus a state-by-state guide to theme parks and amusement parks.

Walt Disney World offers brochures and wonderful materials for teachers. Write to: Walt Disney World Co., P.O. Box 10,000, Lake Buena Vista, FL 32830-1000. Request a catalog.

My Theme Park

A Great Place to Visit

You are so special and amazing that your home town or state has decided to set aside land for a theme park in your honor! Five acres will be reserved for you to transform into a place that reflects who you are. You get to name it, design it, and dictate park policy. It's a place where you'll be the Number One V.I.P. (Very Important Person) every day! As you plan your theme park, consider the following questions. Jot down answers, ideas, and preliminary sketches on separate sheets of paper.

Once you are finished planning your theme park, you will build a scale model using found or recycled materials. Start collecting materials as soon as possible. As you decide what attractions and activities your park will offer, try to think in terms of what you will use to represent them on your scale model.

1 What will you call your theme park? Will you name it after you, or after one of your special interests, characteristics, or abilities? Brainstorm a list of possibilities. The name you choose might inspire some attractions or activities.

2 Where will your theme park be? Think about your home town or state, then choose your location carefully. Will there be water nearby? Hills or mountains? Desert? Beaches? A forest or woods? In a remote area or near a city? Give reasons for your choice of location.

3 What will be the purpose of your theme park? Fun and games? A quiet, meditative experience? Exciting adventures? Will the activities and attractions be "left-brained" or "right-brained"? (Left-brained activities include reading, writing, and talking. Right-brained activities include creativity, imagination, spatial tasks, dreaming, and music.) Write a statement of purpose for your park.

My Theme Park

---

4 What will your theme park look like? Will it be filled with sculptures, bright colors, and daring architecture, or will it be more subtle, natural, and in tune with the environment? Will it be old-fashioned? Modern? Futuristic? Set in a particular historical period? Will it tell your life story? Write a description of how your park will look.

5 What attractions and activities will your theme park offer? What will visitors see or do? Brainstorm a list of possibilities. Give each attraction or activity a name and briefly describe it. Underline or star major attractions. You will want to give visitors many choices of things to do. Be sure to consider the location and year-round climate. Will some attractions be indoors? Which ones will be outdoors?

6 What services will your theme park offer? Will there be places to eat a picnic lunch and rest for a while? What about concession stands? Gift shops? A lost-and-found? A first-aid station? How will you keep your theme park clean? Will you have specially designed trash containers? Will there be containers for recycling?

7 What will be the layout of your theme park? Will it be a logical, orderly grid, with everything readily accessible and easy to find? Or will it be a puzzle and a challenge to figure out? (Remember that your theme park should reflect *you*.) Describe your layout and create some preliminary sketches.

8 Using graph paper or large drawing paper, create a detailed map of your theme park. Use symbols and colors to indicate the various attractions, activities, and services. List them on a key for explanation. Keep the scale of your park in mind.

9 What will be the policies and rules of your theme park? Will any reflect your personality and interests? For example, if you are a night owl, will your park stay open late, and will admission fees be lower after 10 p.m.? If you like animals, will pets be allowed? Be creative and specific. Include general admission fees for adults, teenagers, and children.

10 What foods and beverages will be available at the refreshment stands? What foods and beverages do you enjoy? Fast foods, health foods, special foods of any kind? (Healthful fast foods?)

11 If you have worked your way through all of the preceding questions, you should be ready to start building your scale model. Perhaps you have already gathered some building materials. Now it is time to follow your plan. Pay special attention to details, and use your best crafts and building skills.

12 While parts of your model are drying, prepare a simple brochure or advertisement for your theme park. Be prepared to explain your finished products (scale model, brochure, advertisement) to your classmates.

The Museum of I

This open-ended creative activity challenges students to seek new means of expressing their identity through the arts and with abstraction, culminating with oral expression of their ideas and products.

   This is a long-range project (4–6 weeks), as it requires a lot of introspection. Allow planning and production time both in class and at home. Schedule a few days for oral presentations. Ideally, this project should be assigned during the second half of the school year, after students have gotten to know each other, bonded, and feel comfortable about being open. Even then, some students may not want to present their projects orally in front of the class. Offer them the option of presenting them to you privately.

Role Performance

Students create an artistic expression to represent the self in an abstract way.

Related Curriculum

Language Arts, Humanities, Art

Learning Objectives

By the end of this project, students will be able to:

- recognize and identify various forms of artistic expression (visual arts, performance, dance and music, literary)
- create a "self-portrait" without reference to any of their physical features or characteristics
- have a better understanding of the "abstract"— that which expresses a quality apart from an object, with little or no pictorial representation
- give an oral presentation (3–7 minutes) of their finished work

Learning Styles

Affective, Individual

Materials Needed

- copies of "The Museum of I: In Search of Self" handout (pages 31–32) for each student

The specific materials needed for this project will vary according to the students' individual plans. It should be up to each student to bring his or her own supplies, although you may want to offer assistance in finding certain items, if necessary. Have the following on hand:

- paints, markers, rulers, tape measures, scissors, assorted papers, hot glue guns, glue sticks, tape, etc. (the basics)
- reproductions of famous portraits
- a supply of 4" x 6" cards

Doing the Project

1. Ask students to bring in photographs of themselves (or take pictures of your own) and display them on a bulletin board, or take slides of your students and present a slide show with music. Explain that photographs are familiar and traditional ways for people to represent themselves. Then introduce the project by telling the students that they are going to be representing themselves in *unfamiliar* and *nontraditional* ways. For this project, they will create representations of themselves that don't look like them but are still "likenesses." They will create *abstract expressions* of themselves.

2. Discuss portraiture and alternatives to representing a person physically. Show reproductions of famous portraits and discuss what qualities they reveal. Ask the students to brainstorm ways they would represent these same people abstractly.

3. Have the students brainstorm ways they might represent *themselves* abstractly. Guide them toward responses that reflect their own talents or means of self-expression. Allow time for much discussion and sharing of ideas. If the students are slow getting started, you might ask questions like the following:

   ▶ Are there any dancers in our class? Who? Are there any singers? Musicians? Poets? Novelists? Short-story writers? Composers?

   ▶ Are there any fashion designers? Chefs? Poets? Painters? Photographers? Playwrights? Woodworkers?

   ▶ Might someone design a computer program to represent himself or herself? Create a recipe? Make a video? Bake and decorate a cake? Draw plans or build a model for a building, a park, or a garden?

   ▶ What are some other ways that a person might represent himself or herself—creatively and abstractly?

4. Distribute "The Museum of I: In Search of Self" handout. Read through it with the students. Answer questions and provide explanations and details as needed. While students are working on their museum projects, be available to offer advice and assistance at each step. It may be most important to just listen and affirm the students as they sort through possibilities and approaches to the project.

5. Schedule the oral presentations. Reserve any necessary space and equipment (audiocassette player, slide projector, movie projector, videocassette player, etc.).

6. Evaluate the students' projects, using the criteria given on the handout.

EXPERIENCE NOTES

Students absolutely love this project! It allows them to choose their favorite activities and explore their favorite subject (themselves), while giving them insights into each other's talents, interests, and selves. Finished works become important as documentation of who they were at a particular point in their lives. When former students return to visit me, they always mention their "Museum of I" projects. The usual comment is, "I think I'll keep that forever."

My students' past projects have included an original ballet, a sonata, a musical slide program, abstract paintings, sculptures from found objects, nesting boxes, dramatic monologues, comedy skits, a model of a circus, a model of a house, a model of a golf course, a tapestry, a comic book, an epic poem, and an original, hand-painted dress decorated with poetry and embroidery.

Expanding on the Project

- Invite guest speakers in the various arts disciplines to share their work and methods of creating.

- Plan to exhibit student projects in a "Museum of I" display, perhaps in the media center. As part of the project, have students prepare a 4" x 6" card giving their name, the title of their work, the media, size, and a brief description or explanation. This card can be used for museum display purposes.

Alternative Project

- Have students create photo collages to represent themselves. Make available plenty of magazines with photographs and illustrations. The students should clip and arrange objects and images (not people) that show "who they are." If possible, begin this project by introducing your students to the Italian artist Giuseppe Arcimboldo. He lived from 1527–1593 and was way ahead of his time. Few people today know his name, but many recognize his famous paintings—still-life portraits using fruits, flowers, books, trees, animals, vegetables, etc. His work still influences artists today. Students absolutely love his surreal art and enjoy trying to imitate his style. In fact, it's easy to find allusions to Arcimboldo's paintings in contemporary food advertisements.

Resources

Feldman, Edmund Burke. *Varieties of Visual Experience*, 4th edition. (New York: Harry N. Abrams, Inc., 1992.) An excellent general resource.

Kreigeskorte, Werner. *Guiseppe Arcimboldo*. (Cologne, West Germany: Benedikt Taschen Verlag, 1988.) Check your country library, interlibrary loan, or a museum library.

Newman, Arnold. *One Mind's Eye*. (Boston: New York Graphic Society, 1974.) A beautiful book of "environmental portraits" of famous people in familiar settings.

Arnold Newman's Americans: National Portrait Gallery, Smithsonian Institution by the National Portrait Gallery, the Smithsonian Institution Staff, Alan Fern, and Arnold Newman. (Boston: Bulfinch Press, 1992.)

THE MUSEUM OF I

In Search of Self

Who are you? There is no other being on Earth exactly like you. Your specific combination of matter and energy is totally unique . . . but rarity is not enough! What else makes you special?

This project challenges you to explore the wonder of you. You'll go where no one has gone before and seek new ways of expressing your own identity.

The Challenge

You are going to create a self-portrait without including any of your physical features or characteristics—the "essence" of yourself in a creative, artistic, abstract form. You will work individually, in class and/or at home. There are no other restrictions on this project. When you are through, you will present your self-portrait to the class and explain why it represents you.

The Steps

1 Choose a way to represent yourself abstractly. You might have had a good idea during the brainstorming you did in class. Or you might need more thinking time to come up with an idea you want to try.

THE MUSEUM OF I

2 Decide what medium you want to work in. You may wish to represent yourself through the visual arts, the performing arts, the literary arts, or some other art form—maybe even one you invent. Your self-portrait can be *anything* you want to create or do.

IMPORTANT

If you have any question about whether your project is realistic and/or suitable, talk to your teacher. Some projects can cause storage problems in the classroom.

3 Create your self-portrait. If you need help along the way, ask the teacher or experts in your area of expression (other dancers, artists, composers, etc.).

4 When you have finished your self-portrait, plan and practice your oral presentation. It should be 3–7 minutes long. Tell your teacher if you will need any special equipment or facilities (audio-visual equipment, performance space, etc.).

5 Prepare a 4" x 6" card (typed or neatly printed) giving your name, the title of your work, the media, the size, and a brief description or explanation. If you are doing performance art, create a poster, playbill, or photograph and attach it to your card.

How Your Project Will Be Evaluated

This project is about self-expression, not artistic talent. Your work will be evaluated using these criteria:

- creativity and originality (how creative? how original?)
- accuracy (is it a true portrait of you? does it reflect you?)
- quality (was it carefully thought out, made, or performed? does it reflect substantial effort on your part?)
- overall impact (is it terrific?).

Your oral presentation and 4" x 6" card will also be considered in your evaluation. Your oral presentation should be interesting and well-planned. Your card should clearly and effectively document your project.

FLASHBACK

In this activity, students choose a period in history that interests them, then "travel back in time" with a ballad or poem that tells about themselves and their own time.

Role Performance

Students compose and perform a ballad or narrative poem.

Related Curriculum

Language Arts, Music, Social Studies, History, Geography

Learning Objectives

By the end of this project, students will be able to:

* research a period in history
* understand the structure, format, and style of ballads and narrative poems
* create a ballad or narrative poem that tells a tale about themselves
* give an oral presentation of their work, including an introduction

Learning Styles

Individual, Affective, Cognitive

Materials Needed

* copies of the "Flashback: Blast into the Past" handout (pages 35–36) for each student
* examples of ballads and narrative poems on recordings and/or in books
* blank audiocassettes and/or videocassettes
* audiocassette and/or videocassette recorder/player
* paints, paper, markers, poster board, etc. for making signs
* an easel for displaying students' signs

Doing the Project

1. Introduce the students to ballads and narrative poems, if you have not already done this in another context. Explain that a ballad is a folk song that tells a dramatic tale, usually in the third person. It often uses vivid dialogue and is composed in *quatrains* (four-line stanzas), *couplets* (two-line stanzas), or six-line stanzas. A narrative poem also tells a story—usually about a historical event or romance.

   Play some musical or spoken word recordings of ballads or narrative poems for the students. Or find printed copies of lyrics and poems to read aloud.

2. Distribute the "Flashback: Blast into the Past" handout. Read through it with the students. Answer questions and provide explanations and details as needed. While students are working on their ballads or poems, be available to offer advice and assistance at each step. Students may need special help understanding the form of a ballad or poem and fitting their words to a rhythm.

3. Schedule the presentations. You may want to prepare the room by arranging the students' desks or tables as if they were in a café.

4. Evaluate the students' projects, or have students evaluate each other's projects. Be sure to applaud each presentation, like any appreciative live audience would.

EXPERIENCE NOTES

Some students who choose to compose ballads will definitely *not* want to sing them in front of the class, either live or on a recording. As options, they might ask other students to perform their ballads for them, or they might "say" them to musical accompaniment. Students who enjoy singing but are shy about performing live before an audience might feel more comfortable videotaping their ballads or poems.

This project can be highly motivating for students who play musical instruments. Some of my students have said, "At last—a project for me!"

Expanding on the Project

■ The results of this project could easily be turned into illustrated books. The books could be created by the individual ballad/poem writers or by small groups.

■ Find out if any students are willing to be "troubadours" and perform for other classes or schools.

Alternative Projects

■ This project can be used as a cooperative learning activity with small groups of three or four. Take a survey to determine the students' skills, talents, and preferences, then try to include a singer, writer, musician, and researcher in each group.

■ Puppetry is another way to express this type of creative output. Construct a simple, portable stage. Have students create backdrop scenery as one of the project requirements.

Resources

Check your library or media center for recordings (musical and/or spoken word) of one or more of these famous ballads and poems:

—"Annabel Lee" (Edgar Allan Poe)

—"The Ballad of the Harp-Weaver" (Edna St. Vincent Millay)

—"Barbara Allen" (Anonymous)

—"Paul Revere's Ride" (Henry Wadsworth Longfellow)

—"Rime of the Ancient Mariner" (Samuel Taylor Coleridge)

—Any "Robin Hood" or "King Arthur" ballad

—"The Village Blacksmith" (Henry Wadsworth Longfellow)

Check your library or media center for recordings by these and other modern-day balladeers:

—Harry Chapin ("Cat's in the Cradle," from *Greatest Stories Live*, Electra, 1976)

—Paul Simon ("Further to Fly," from *Paul Simon 1964/1993*, Warner Brothers, 1993)

—Jackson Browne (*World in Motion*, Electra, 1989)

Henson, Cheryl. *The Muppets Make Puppets*. (New York: Workman Publishing, 1994.) The absolute best puppet book ever!

Flashback

Blast into the Past

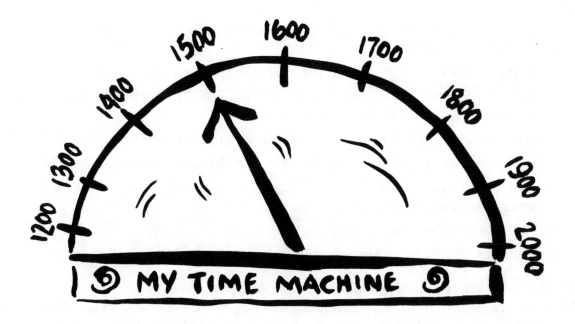

Through some mysterious time warp, you've been flashed back to the past. You're suddenly a traveling troubadour with a mandolin in Medieval England or Renaissance Italy . . . or a poet who goes from town to town, bearing stories and tales . . . or a guitar-playing folk singer on a San Francisco street corner . . . or a "beat poet" in a New York café (cool, daddy-o!). You have your audience's attention. What will be your song? What tale will you choose to tell? What will you want your audience to know about you and your own time period?

1 Choose a time period in history that interests you, or a period when you think people could have used some wisdom from the future. (It may be easier for you to start by choosing an important event from history, then deciding what you might say to people just before or during the event.)

2 Choose a theme or message for your ballad or narrative poem. What would you like to tell the people of that time? If you knew they would listen, what would you say? Would you relate a story about yourself? A tale about our times?

3 Choose a style for your ballad or narrative poem.

- Will it be heroic? (sweeping, grand, and dramatic, with heroes and heroines, monsters and gods)
- Will it be comic? (witty and amusing, with silly characters and events)
- Will it be tragic? (dark and foreboding, with a series of events that leads to a terrible end for someone or something)
- Will it be blasé? (smooth, sophisticated, worldly, unemotional)
- Will it be questioning? (thought-provoking, challenging, inspiring)
- Will it be autobiographical? (your life story, or an event from your life with a message for your audience)
- Will it be prophetic? (foretelling the future)
- Will it be _____? (what's your style?)

4 Decide on a story to tell in your ballad or narrative poem. Write a first draft in story form (simple sentences, paragraphs, dialogue). Write a second draft in ballad or poem form. Rhyme only if you want to, and only if you can. Your ballad or poem doesn't have to rhyme.

5 Prepare and practice an oral presentation of your ballad or poem. You might choose to sing it or say it. You might ask someone else to sing it or say it for you. You might want to present your ballad or poem live, or make an audio or video recording. If you have written a ballad, you may want to set it to music—original music or music by another artist. If you use another artist's music, be sure to give credit to the artist.

6 Prepare a visual showing clothing from your chosen historical period to set the scene. You might make a drawing, poster, collage, or overhead transparency. If possible, it would be fun to dress in the appropriate clothing. Or would you prefer to "travel through time" in the type of clothing you wear today?

7 Prepare a sign showing the month, date, year, and location of your "visit." Be creative! Maybe you can find some examples of signs from that historic period and use the same lettering style. Prop your sign on an easel for your presentation.

HOT-AIR BALLOON

No matter how "high-tech" our world becomes, we will always be fascinated by beautiful hot-air balloons. This activity gives students the opportunity to explore the world of hot-air ballooning as they design a balloon and plan an imaginary voyage.

Role Performance

Students design a hot-air balloon and plan a voyage.

Related Curriculum

Language Arts, Science, Art, Geography, Math

Learning Objectives

By the end of this project, students will be able to:

- appreciate the hot-air balloon as a mode of travel
- understand the scientific principles involved in hot-air ballooning
- design a personal hot-air balloon
- create a detailed drawing or model of their balloon
- create a map and an itinerary

Learning Styles

Affective, Cognitive, Individual

Materials Needed

- copies of the "Hot-Air Balloon: Flight of Imagination" handout (pages 40–41) for each student
- videos, articles, books, brochures, visuals, etc. about hot-air balloons and ballooning
- large pieces of white drawing paper
- colored pencils, crayons, and/or fine-line felt-tipped pens or markers
- assorted materials for creating models (optional)

Doing the Project

1. Introduce the project by showing a video or film about hot-air ballooning, such as *Around the World in Eighty Days*. Pass around brochures, articles, and visuals. Any balloon resources will do, but some are necessary for visual input, since actual contact with this sport is limited.

2. Discuss the scientific principles that keep hot-air balloons aloft. Scientifically minded students may wish to research this and make a presentation for the class.

3. Give students a brief ballooning "experience" with an imagination exercise. Have them sit comfortably, close their eyes, relax, and breathe deeply as you read the following. Pause between sentences.

   "It's a gorgeous morning. The sun is coming up bright and beautiful, there's a wonderful breeze, and the clouds are white and full against a bright blue sky. All conditions are perfect for your first hot-air ballooning experience. You greet your companions and begin to load your provisions. See yourself checking the gear, climbing into the basket, and settling in, ready for the thrill of a lifetime. You make the necessary departure preparations and suddenly you are airborne, lifting higher and higher. Up into the sky. Floating silently, up and up. The land seems to shrink beneath you as the colorful balloon reaches for the clouds. Feel the air around you as you swirl to unknown heights and float across the landscape. Except for the occasional whoosh of the burner heating the air in the balloon, and the creak of the ropes, and quiet conversation, it's absolutely silent. You can even hear sounds from the ground below—cows mooing, cars, people calling 'Hello!' as they notice you and wave."

   Let the students enjoy this experience for a few minutes, then ask them to gently open their eyes. Most will be smiling. Invite them to talk about how they felt during the imagination exercise. They may want to write their thoughts in their journals and share them with the group.

4. Distribute the "Hot-Air Balloon: Flight of Imagination" handout. Read through it with the students. Answer questions and provide explanations and details as needed. While students are working on their hot-air balloons and maps, be available to offer advice and assistance at each step.

5. Evaluate the students' projects, or have students evaluate their own or each other's projects.

EXPERIENCE NOTES

Students love the whole concept of hot-air ballooning, which appeals to adventurers and "romantics" alike. Most students will want to make models of their balloons, so look for a variety of materials. Small, square produce containers and cube-shaped cardboard tissue boxes are good for the basket. Thin, solid-colored fabric (muslin) or plastic will work for a balloon, but must be painted with acrylic or fabric paint. Permanent markers are also effective.

The math challenge will be designing a pattern for the balloon. If you have access to a set of Tangrams, students might use these as templates to create designs.

For inspiration, I like to play the recording "Up, Up and Away" by the Fifth Dimension on the first day of this project.

Expanding on the Project

- Students may enjoy reading novels about ballooning, such as *The Twenty-One Balloons* and *By Balloon to the Sahara*.

- Contact a local hot-air ballooning club or organization. Invite one of the members to visit your class, talk about ballooning, and show slides.

Alternative Projects

■ Divide the class into small groups to research information on famous hot-air balloons, blimps, or dirigibles.

■ This activity could also be adapted to different themes—ships, trains, ultralight aircraft, off-road vehicles, etc. Adapt the student handout, gather appropriate resources, and follow the same process.

Resources

Around the World in Eighty Days. A 1956 Oscar-winning feature film starring David Niven and Shirley MacLaine, based on the book by Jules Verne and available on video.

Du Bois, William Pene. *The Twenty-One Balloons.* (New York: Puffin Books, 1986.) This book won the prestigious Newbery Medal.

Johnson, Neil. *Fire and Silk: Flying in a Hot Air Balloon.* (New York: Little, Brown, 1991). Majestic photographs record a hot-air balloon flight from inflation to pack-up.

Macaulay, David. *The Way Things Work.* (Boston: Houghton-Mifflin, 1988), page 113.

Terman, Douglas. *By Balloon to the Sahara.* (New York: Bantam Books, Inc., 1989.) This book was written for younger readers, so you'll need to decide if it's appropriate for your class. (If some of your students already know this book, you might present it as "nostalgia reading"—a chance to look back at a book they enjoyed when they were younger.)

Most encyclopedias feature comprehensive articles on the hows and whys of hot-air ballooning. Borrow recent volumes from the school media center, or arrange to spend a class period there. Information on ballooning is also found in some CD-ROM encyclopedias.

Many cities, counties, and states hold annual hot-air balloon festivals and rallies. Three of the biggest are in New Mexico, Wisconsin, and Iowa. Write or call for more information:

—Albuquerque International Balloon Fiesta, 8309 Washington Place Northeast, Albuquerque, NM 87113; (505) 821-1000. If you happen to live in or near Albuquerque, perhaps you can take a class trip to this spectacle, held each October.

—Great Wisconsin Dells Balloon Rally, c/o Visitors and Convention Bureau, Box 390, 701 Superior Street, Wisconsin Dells, WI 53965; (608) 254-8088 or 1-800-22-DELLS (1-800-223-3557). Held late each spring.

—National Balloon Classic, P.O. Box 346, Indianola, IA 51025; (515) 961-8415. (This is also the address for the Balloon Federation of America, listed below.)

The following organizations have information on ballooning:

—Balloon Federation of America, P.O. Box 346, Indianola, IA 50125.

—Bombard Balloon Adventures, 6727 Curran Street, McClean, VA 22101-6006; toll-free telephone 1-800-862-8537. Bombard will send brochures and loan a video about ballooning.

—National Balloon Museum, 1601 North Jefferson, P.O. Box 149, Indianola, IA 51025; (515) 961-3714.

—For mood music, try the Fifth Dimension's "Up, Up and Away" (*Gold Medal Collection,* Rhino, 1988).

Hot-Air Balloon

Flight of Imagination

You are about to design your very own hot-air balloon and plan your first flight. You may decide to create an actual model of your balloon. Hopefully, you'll get "carried away"!

1 Consider these questions. Write your responses, notes, and sketches on a separate sheet of paper. Elaborate on your thoughts and ideas.

- ■ What will my balloon look like?
- ■ What will I name my balloon?
- ■ Where will I go in my balloon?
- ■ Who will I invite to go with me?
- ■ What tangible things will I bring? (food? water? a radio?)
- ■ What "intangible" things will I bring? (Think abstractly.)

Hot-Air Balloon

---

* How often will I use my balloon?
* What worries, if any, will I have about my balloon? What will I do to relieve my worries and find peace of mind?
* What adventures might I have?
* How will I handle an emergency, if one should happen?
* How will I document my balloon rides, if at all?

2 Design and draw your own personal hot-air balloon. It should be highly individualized and reflect your preferences and style. Include some or all of these elements in your design:

color(s)   name(s)   illustration(s)   motif(s)

logo(s)   slogan(s)   pattern(s)   scene(s)

3 Plan a simple itinerary for an imaginary journey in your hot-air balloon. Where will you go? What stops will you make? (These decisions may influence the tangible and intangible things you decide to bring.)

4 Draw a physical map of the route you will take. Will you fly over land, valleys, deserts, meadows, ice fields, islands, volcanoes, rivers, lakes, oceans, mountains, farms, small towns, cities? What land forms will you want to see? Show the features and highlights of your route on a simple map, using appropriate colors. Indicate the path of your balloon with a dotted line. Note points of interest with symbols or drawings.

5 Add another creative element to this project—anything you choose—in any way you wish.

Bon Voyage and Happy Landing!

I Am a Puzzle

"Fitting in" seems to worry most young people in all situations. They often feel like a puzzle piece that's turned the wrong way, or even as if they're in the wrong puzzle altogether! This project allows students to examine those "puzzling" feelings and to ultimately see that they are indeed part of a wonderful picture—their own unique lives.

Role Performance

Students create a puzzle.

Related Curriculum

Language Arts, Math, Art, Multiculturalism

Learning Objectives

By the end of this project, students will be able to:
* create an original puzzle with themselves as a central theme
* think flexibly and abstractly
* exhibit elaboration and originality
* exhibit crafts skills

Learning Styles

Affective, Cooperative, Individual

Materials Needed

* copies of the "I Am A Puzzle: The Pieces of My Life" handout (pages 45–46) for each student
* large sheets of white paper for sketching
* newsprint or old (recycled) paper for making patterns
* carbon paper for transferring patterns
* assorted pieces of cardboard, poster board, and/or recycled file folders, or pieces of wood
* strong, sharp scissors and/or X-acto knives (mat knives)
* a jigsaw, if thicker wood is used
* sandpaper, if wood is used
* permanent markers and/or acrylic paints
* materials for decorating the puzzles, such as pictures (from magazines), scraps of fancy papers, gift wraps, and/or fabrics, glitter, buttons, stickers, etc.
* rubber cement or white glue
* materials for framing the final puzzles
* large manila envelopes or resealable plastic bags for puzzle storage

Doing the Project

1. For younger students, or as a "get-acquainted" activity, purchase or make a large blank jigsaw puzzle with large puzzle pieces. Give each student one puzzle piece. Explain that they will decorate their pieces to clearly represent themselves, *without* drawing self-portraits. They can use any of the available supplies. Encourage use of representative textures and designs. Tell them to be careful not to change or damage the connecting edges, so that when everyone has finished, the class can cooperatively assemble the puzzle. Preserving this display all year will be a meaningful reminder to the students to celebrate their differences.

2. Introduce the project by telling the students that they are going to make whole puzzles representing themselves and their lives. Their puzzle will make a statement about their unique talents, traits, interests, history, favorites, family, friends, etc. They can include whatever information they're willing to reveal in order to express "who they are" in puzzle form. Encourage divergent thinking about puzzle shapes and the use of negative (blank) spaces. Not all puzzles (or people!) are square.

3. Distribute the "I Am a Puzzle: The Pieces of My Life" handout. Read through it with the students. Answer questions and provide explanations and details as needed. While students are working on their puzzles, be available to offer advice and assistance at each step.

4. When the puzzles are finished, have the students present them to the class. They can simply show their puzzles, or they can show them and offer explanations of various pieces. Let them choose the approach they prefer. Have a class discussion about the puzzles. You may want to focus on individual puzzles and ask questions like these:

    ◗ What does this puzzle reveal about the person who made it?

    ◗ Are there any surprises? Any revelations?

    ◗ Does the puzzle raise any questions? Does it answer any questions?

Expand the discussion into the area of puzzles as metaphors, using ideas from the student handout and other ideas contributed by the students. You might offer the following:

   ◗ Life is a giant jigsaw puzzle.

   ◗ Sometimes it's hard to know where we fit in.

   ◗ Each piece is important to completing the puzzle.

5. Evaluate the students' projects, or have students evaluate each other's projects.

EXPERIENCE NOTES

This project is an excellent opportunity for introspection and creative expression. I have heard comments like, "My self-puzzle has a missing piece because I'm not complete yet." I have seen students become intense about selecting "just the right" texture, shape, or color to clearly represent Mom, Dad, or themselves.

Allow students to help each other cut out the puzzle pieces. If you have access to a woodshop class, the students or teacher there may be willing to help your students cut puzzle pieces out of wood.

Expanding on the Project

▪ Before introducing this project, have students work together on a large jigsaw puzzle. Someone may want to bring in an old favorite. Direct the students to notice puzzle piece shapes, pattern repetitions, design details, and level of difficulty. More importantly, let them just enjoy working together to complete the puzzle.

▪ Read Shel Silverstein's wonderful book, *The Missing Piece*.

Alternative Project

- Study the work of M.C. Escher, the Dutch graphic artist and mathematician who was a master at visual puzzles. Today, many jigsaw puzzles are produced using his complex designs.

Resources

Silverstein, Shel. *The Missing Piece*. (New York: HarperCollins Children's Books, 1976.)

There is an abundance of materials available on the art of M.C. Escher. Some examples:

— *M.C. Escher: His Life and Complete Graphic Work*. (New York: Abrams, 1982.) Includes the story of the artist's life (with virtually his entire correspondence), a comprehensive catalog of his graphic works, and over 600 illustrations, including 36 color plates.

— Films about Escher on video include *Adventures in Perception* and *The Fantastic World of M.C. Escher*. (For help in finding videos to purchase, call Video Trackers, 1-800-718-4336, or Vidco Finders, 1-800-343-4727.)

— *Art & Man* Magazine, Vol. 22, No. 3, December 1991–January 1992. Titled "M.C. Escher: Optical Art," the entire issue focuses on Escher. *Art & Man* is published by Scholastic under the direction of The National Gallery of Art. Special teachers' edition and quantity subscription discounts are available. Write to: ART & MAN, Scholastic Inc., 2931 East McCarty Street, P.O. Box 3710, Jefferson City, MO 65102-9957. Back issues may be available in your school or local library on microfilm or microfiche.

— Calendars, cards, puzzles, posters—even scarves, socks, and ties—featuring Escher's graphic works are available in stores.

Stave Puzzle Manufacturers. Stave puzzles are expensive to purchase, but the company will send you a hand-crafted wooden puzzle piece and a catalog that is very inspiring for puzzle-makers. Write or call: Stave Puzzle Manufacturers, P.O. Box 329, Norwich, VT 05055; (802) 295-5200.

I Am a Puzzle

The Pieces of My Life

Life often feels like a giant jigsaw puzzle. Perhaps you're the missing piece, looking for your space. Maybe you know you're the corner piece—the one that gets everything started. Maybe you're the last piece people notice, yet they can't finish without you.

You're going to design and create a puzzle that represents you and your life. This puzzle will be different from any puzzle you have ever seen. There is no "boxtop picture" to copy or follow. Your puzzle will be unique in the world. Each shape and pattern will have a specific meaning to you.

1 Use these questions to start thinking about and planning your puzzle. Jot down notes, ideas, sketches, and elaborations as you consider each question.

- ▤ If life really was a giant jigsaw puzzle, what would your piece look like? What size, shape, color(s), and texture(s) would it be?

- ▤ Which pieces would connect to your piece?

- ▤ Which pieces would be far away from your piece?

- ▤ Which pieces might have difficulty "fitting in" or "fitting together"? (Think metaphorically.)

- ▤ Which pieces would be similar? Which would be different? Would some pieces be identical? Would some pieces be very different from the others?

- ▤ Would other pieces be simpler or more complex than your piece?

I Am a Puzzle

2 Create your puzzle.

- Start by making a sketch of your puzzle. Experiment with different shapes for individual puzzle pieces.

- When you have the shapes you like on paper, make a pattern for your puzzle. Transfer your pattern to cardboard, wood, or whatever you will use to make your puzzle.

- Carefully cut out your puzzle pieces with scissors, an X-acto knife, or a jigsaw. Sand the pieces if necessary, without altering the shapes.

- Use any available materials—paint, markers, crayons, fabric, pictures from magazines, glitter, etc.—to decorate your pieces and convey the meaning of each piece. Try different textures. Experiment with collage.

- Determine a way to create a frame-board or "packaging" for your puzzle.

3 Write a brief description or explanation of your puzzle. What do the various pieces, colors, textures, designs, etc. mean to you? Can you see how you complete the puzzle of your life? Can you see how others need to relate to the piece that is you . . . and how you need to relate to them?

Personal Quotation Journal

This activity expands into a lifelong pursuit and becomes a treasured possession for students (or adults) who embrace the importance of forming a personal philosophy of life.

Role Performance

Students select quotations for a personal permanent collection.

Related Curriculum

Language Arts, Humanities, Social Studies

Learning Objectives

By the end of this project, students will be able to:
* use books of quotations and quotation indexes
* correctly copy quotations
* use critical thinking to select quotations

Learning Styles

Affective, Cognitive, Individual

Materials Needed

* copies of the "Personal Quotation Journal: This Says What I Feel" handout (pages 50–51) for each student
* numerous books of quotations
* student journals—inexpensive notebooks, bound blank books, or booklets students make in class
* felt-tipped calligraphy pens (optional)

Doing the Project

1. To introduce this activity, it would be especially helpful and inspiring if you had a personal quotation journal to share with the students. At best, this will be a special hardcover book that implies its importance to you. If you don't have a personal quotation journal, you may want to do this project yourself and start one.

2. Have available a wide variety of books of quotations to show the students.

   ❧ Call attention to books geared to specific topics—quotations by women, humorous quotations, quotations for public speakers, and so on. Invite the students to browse through the books with you.

   ❧ Demonstrate how to use the indexes to find quotations on specific topics and quotations by specific authors.

   ❧ Point out that each collection is organized somewhat differently. Some are alphabetical by author; some are alphabetical by subject; some are chronological.

   ❧ Challenge the students to look up examples and share them orally.

3. Distribute the "Personal Quotation Journal: This Says What I Feel" handout. Read through it with the students. Answer questions and provide explanations and details as needed. While students are working on their journals, be available to offer advice and assistance at each step. Encourage students to be selective in the quotations they choose.

   Students may add personally meaningful quotations from other sources—magazines, T-shirts, billboards, favorite songs, political speeches, people they know, other books they have read—but an important part of this project is learning how to use reference books of quotations, so at least some of the entries in their journals should be drawn from those.

4. Evaluate the students' projects. Evaluation criteria might include:

   ❧ the total number of quotations (at least 15)

   ❧ how well the quotations express the student's personal philosophy

   ❧ neatness

   ❧ completeness (are sources cited?)

   ❧ creativity

   ❧ variety of subjects

   ❧ variety of sources.

EXPERIENCE NOTES

Students love to discover humorous or profound quotations and read them aloud to their friends. During and after this project, they often begin to bring in other quotations they find in books they are reading, and quotations they have heard on television or radio shows. For many students, collecting quotations becomes a treasure hunt— and a lifelong passion.

Expanding on the Project

▪ Students can use their collected quotations to create dramatic presentations—monologues, skits, or puppet shows. If many of their quotations come from a favorite person, they might dress up as this individual and recite his or her most interesting, meaningful, and/or memorable quotations.

▪ Have students create their own journals from scratch—selecting the paper, making the covers, and binding the journals.

▪ Have students write to public figures, local celebrities, sports figures, city and state officials, and others to request their favorite quotations. The letters can become a special classroom collection.

Alternative Projects

- Some students enjoy studying calligraphy while collecting quotations. Copying a quotation in calligraphy in one's journal seems to give it even more importance. Have students select their favorite quotations to write in their best calligraphy on special paper. Display the quotations on a bulletin board.

- Students who enjoy using computers can create special treatments of favorite quotations, using borders, various type fonts, dingbats, graphics, and other elements.

- The medieval art of illuminating letters is fascinating to students with artistic interests. Provide special paper, colored pencils, and markers for students who want to try their hand at illuminating letters. (Future written assignments may have elaborately drawn first letters!)

Resources

Most libraries and media centers have large collections of books of quotations. In addition to the standards—*Bartlett's Familiar Quotations, The Oxford Dictionary of Quotations, The Columbia Dictionary of Quotations,* Bergen Evans's *Dictionary of Quotations,* and others—you will want to gather books of quotations by women, quotations on humor, modern quotations, and so on. There are big books of quotations, and smaller books devoted to special topics (writing, love, medicine, music, art, business, law, and so on). Try to have a wide variety of books to show your students. A few suggestions:

- Maggio, Rosalie. *The Beacon Book of Quotations by Women.* (Boston: Beacon Press, 1992.)

- Metcalf, Fred. *The Penguin Dictionary of Modern Humorous Quotations.* (New York: Viking Penguin, 1988.)

- *The New York Public Library Book of 20th-Century American Quotations,* edited by Stephen Donadio, Joan Smith, Susan Mesner, and Rebecca Davison. (New York: Warner Books/The Stonesong Press, Inc., 1992.)

- *Respectfully Quoted: A Dictionary of Quotations from the Library of Congress,* edited by Suzy Platt. (Washington, D.C.: Congressional Quarterly Inc., 1992.)

- Simpson, James B. *Webster's Two Contemporary Quotations.* (Boston: Houghton Mifflin Co., 1992.)

PERSONAL QUOTATION JOURNAL

This Says What I Feel

Did you ever try to explain a thought or idea and find that the words just didn't sound right? Perhaps you wished that someone else could say it for you. In fact, someone else can, once you learn to use books of quotations and their indexes.

You are about to begin a Personal Quotation Journal—a collection of quotations you find and choose to collect because they say what you feel.

1 Browse through several books of quotations. Notice how they are divided into categories or sections. Notice how they often have extensive indexes. For each book, try to find a quotation in each category or section, so you can become familiar with how the book is organized. When you feel that you have a good understanding of how to use books of quotations, go on to the next step.

2 Select at least 15 quotations to use in your Personal Quotation Journal. For each quotation, ask yourself these questions:

Does it reflect my personal philosophy?

Does this quotation have special meaning to me?

Does it capture a feeling or belief that is true and important for me?

Are these "golden words"?

If you can answer "yes" to one or more of these questions, the quotation *may* be right for your journal. Don't hurry through the selection process. Take your time.

PERSONAL QUOTATION JOURNAL

3 Think of categories for your quotations. (*Examples:* "Friends," "Love," "Family Life," "Humor," "Education," "Coping," "Dreams.") Copy the quotations into your Personal Quotation Journal—a special notebook, bound blank book, or book you make yourself. Give each section a title (category) and group the quotations within the sections. Leave plenty of space between sections to add quotations you find in the future.

- Copy the quotations neatly, carefully, and accurately.

- Use calligraphy or special lettering, if you like.

- For each quotation, credit the author. Write the author's name after the quotation, along with the source of the quotation (a speech? a play? a novel? an interview?). Write the title of the book in which you found the quotation; if you found it somewhere else (a radio program, favorite novel, magazine, etc.), give details.

   Here is an example of how you might credit a quotation:

   "Friendship with oneself is all-important, because without it one cannot be friends with anyone else in the world."
   —Eleanor Roosevelt in Ladies' Home Journal (1944): found in
   The Beacon Book of Quotations by Women, compiled by Rosalie Maggio.

4 If you feel especially inspired, add three *original* quotations—words by you that others might quote someday (or already do).

Garden of Insights

Role Performance

Students create a plan for a garden.

Related Curriculum

Language Arts, Science, Math, Art

Learning Objectives

By the end of this project, students will be able to:

- research various plants, flowers, and vegetables
- draw a plan for a garden
- understand metaphor and simile
- be familiar with basic gardening terminology

Learning Styles

Affective, Cognitive, Individual

Materials Needed

- copies of "Garden of Insights: How Does My Garden Grow?" handout (pages 55–56) for each student
- books, magazines, catalogs, and brochures about gardens and gardening, including some with sample plans and layouts
- large sheets of paper or newsprint for sketching garden plans
- a roll of craft paper (blue is fun, reminding one of "blueprints"), cut into large pieces (18" x 24" or 24" x 24"), or brown paper grocery bags, cut open and flattened
- masking tape to anchor paper to table
- materials for drawing—pens and inks, oil pastels (best), tempera paints, colored pencils
- rulers and yardsticks
- rubber bands for securing rolled-up plans

Doing the Project

1. Introduce the project by asking if there are any gardeners in the room. Has anyone ever tried growing plants, flowers, or vegetables? Does anyone have a house plant in his or her room at home? Many students will have grown bean plants in milk cartons as a school project some-time during elementary school. This counts as "gardening" experience!

   Explain that for this project, everyone will design an imaginary garden that reflects their abilities, interests, feelings, knowledge, dreams, problems, preferences . . . anything they choose to reveal about themselves.

2. Show examples of garden plans and layouts. These are usually aerial views and simply drawn. Most gardening books, magazines, and catalogs include sample plans and layouts.

3. Distribute the "Garden of Insights: How Does My Garden Grow?" handout. Read through it with the students. Answer questions and provide explanations and details as needed. While students are working on their garden plans, be available to offer advice and assistance at each step. Students may need special help measuring their gardens, drawing their plans to scale, and/or creating symbols to represent plants, flowers, vegetables, seating, etc.

4. Evaluate the students' projects, or have the students evaluate each other's projects. Let your classroom become a "Garden of Insights" and bloom with a display of the garden plans.

EXPERIENCE NOTES

One student who "always felt closed in, lacking freedom in her life" created her garden in a terrarium. Another intentionally surrounded his with weeds of incredible variety. This project can truly give insights into students' personalities. Inevitably, some students will want to create their gardens at home. By all means, encourage them—and ask for photos!

This project is especially appropriate for Earth Day (April 22).

Expanding on the Project

- Invite a knowledgeable gardener to visit your class as a guest speaker. Your community probably has a garden club with members who would be delighted to visit and even show slides. This would inspire students and give them a working knowledge of "gardening jargon." Other possibilities for speakers include a landscape architect, someone who works at a nursery, or someone who works at a garden supplies store.

- Have the students create three-dimensional scale models of the gardens they design.

- Take a field trip to a local public garden, conservatory, arboretum, or park with plantings.

- See if your school will permit your class to plant a garden. Take a class vote on which student plan to use, or combine elements from several plans. Depending on the size of your class and the gardening space you have available, you may want to give each student a small section of your garden to plant however he or she chooses.

- Students with a special interest in gardening may be interested in joining a national organization dedicated to helping people become successful gardeners. For information, write or call the National Gardening Association.

Alternative Projects

- Have students design and create terrariums with the same objectives.

- If there is a significant public garden, park, or conservatory in your area, have students visit, research, and report on it. Questions to consider include:

  - Who started it? Why? (Was it begun in memory of an important person or historic event? Is there anything that reflects the person or event?)

  - Does it have a theme or special meaning? (For example, the International Peace Garden in North Dakota and Canada recognizes the long, amicable relationship between the two nations.)

  - What are its special features?

  - Are there fountains and statues? Who created them?

Resources

You will find many books on gardens and gardening in your local library. You may want to start with a volume or two from the *Time-Life Complete Gardener* series. (Alexandria, VA: Time-Life Books, 1995).

Kids in Bloom, Eco-Renewal, P.O. Box 344, Zionsville, IN 46077; (317)-290-6996. Deals in "heirloom" seeds; packages seeds for young people, with history information, instructions, and tips. Request a seed catalog.

National Gardening Association, 180 Flynn Avenue, Burlington, VT 05401; (802) 863-1308. Young people can join this organization; teachers can request information about resources.

Collect brochures and information from famous gardens and parks. Examples:

- Boston Public Garden, Boston, Massachusetts; (617) 522-1966
- Callaway Gardens and Day Butterfly Center, Pine Mountain, Georgia; (404) 663-2281
- Cantigny, Wheaton, Illinois; (708) 668-5161
- Central Park, New York, New York; (212) 397-3156
- Golden Gate Park, San Francisco, California; (415) 666-7200
- Green Animals Topiary Gardens, Portsmouth, Rhode Island; (401) 847-1000
- International Peace Garden, North Dakota and Canada; (701) 263-4390
- Longwood Gardens, Kennet Square, Pennsylvania; (215) 388-6741
- Mitchell Park Conservatory, "The Domes," Milwaukee, Wisconsin; (414) 649-9800
- U.S. National Arboretum, Washington, D.C.; (202) 475-4815

Collect seed catalogs. Any good book on gardening should list several possibilities, with toll-free 800 numbers.

GARDEN OF INSIGHTS

How Does My Garden Grow?

Think of yourself as a plot of land. You will cultivate this land through creativity and imagination and turn it into a garden that reflects who you are. Anyone who sees your garden will learn about your feelings, interests, talents, abilities, preferences, dreams, problems, likes, dislikes, friends, family, and anything else you choose to reveal. Your garden should reflect you as the person you are in the here and now.

1 Any good gardener starts with a plan. As you think about your garden plan, consider the following questions. Think abstractly; the elements of your garden should be similes and metaphors for you and your life. Jot down answers, thoughts, and ideas on paper. Elaborate and give details.

- What shape and size will my garden be?

- Where will it be located? In sun or shade? On hilly land or flat land? Will it be on more than one level?

- What will I grow in my garden? Flowers? Herbs? Vegetables? Wildflowers? Weeds? Trees? A combination of some or all of these?

- Will my garden change as the seasons change? How? Will it bloom year round? Will it have annuals, perennials, or both?

Garden of Insights

- Will I plant my garden sparsely or cover every inch? Will I let things grow wild?

- What colors will be in my garden? Or will it be monochromatic—just one color? (What are the "colors" in your life?)

- What fragrances will my garden have, if any? (Flowers? Herbs?)

- Will I need any special materials to grow my garden? (Tools, plants, seeds?)

- Will my garden have birds or animals living in it? If so, what kinds? How will I attract birds or animals to my garden?

- Will my garden have pests? If so, what kinds? (Who or what are the "pests" in your life?)

- Will my garden have weeds? (Who or what are the "weeds" in your life?)

- Who will visit my garden? What about my garden will be outstanding, remarkable, or especially interesting to visitors?

- Will I play music in my garden to help it thrive? What kind(s) of music will I play?

- Will my garden have walking paths or special places to sit?

- Will my garden have fountains? Statues? Bird baths? Sun dials? Sculptures?

2 Using gardening books, magazines, catalogs, and brochures for inspiration, plan a layout of your garden on paper. (An aerial view works best.) Use symbols and colors to indicate the various plants, areas, and decorative elements of your garden. List them on a key for explanation.

Be creative, use your imagination, and have fun, but keep in mind that the purpose of your garden is to reflect who you are.

Under My Mask

For this project, students explore the "inner" and "outer" faces of their personalities and create transformation masks to depict both sides. Prior to making their masks, they learn about the traditional transformation masks made by the Kwakiutl Indians of the Northwest Coast.

Role Performance

Students make a transformation mask.

Related Curriculum

Language Arts, Social Studies, Art, Humanities

Learning Objectives

By the end of this project, students will be able to:

* use different materials flexibly and creatively

* generate a variety of ideas for modern transformation masks

* create a personal transformation mask that reveals something about themselves

* understand the Kwakiutl Indian belief about transformation and relate it to their own mask-making

Learning Styles

Affective, Cognitive, Individual

Materials Needed

* copies of "Under My Mask—I Am Amazing" (pages 60–61) for each student

* visuals and reference materials on Northwest Coast Kwakiutl Indians, especially information on transformation masks

* assorted "found" or recycled objects from packaging, such as cardboard, molded plastics, cardboard tubes, old poster board, natural materials, shoe boxes, egg cartons, etc.

* scissors

* adhesives and fasteners: rubber cement, masking tape, string, staples, paper fasteners, rubber bands

* acrylic or tempera paints, especially in the traditional Northwest Coast colors of red, black, white, brown, blue, and green

* small objects for decorating the masks, such as bits of yarn, fabrics, fibers, feathers, etc.

* papier-mâché mixture (optional): one part white glue to one part water; strips of newspaper or brown paper towel

Doing the Project

1. Introduce the project by telling the students that they are going to make special masks called "transformation masks." Use questions like the following to begin a discussion:

   ▶ Have you ever wished that you could change your face?

   ▶ Do you sometimes feel as if the face you show to the world isn't the "real you"?

   ▶ Is the "outer you" different from the "inner you"? In what way or ways?

   ▶ Is there value in sometimes showing the "inner you"? Can you give an example of a time when this might be important or helpful?

2. Read aloud the following brief introduction to the Kwakiutl Indians and transformation masks. Present visuals showing examples of transformation masks.

   "The Kwakiutl (Kwaa-kee-U-tull) Indians of America's Northwest Coast and British Columbia's Southwest Coast believe that in the beginning, all animals appeared as humans. Then the spirit Transformer changed each one into a particular species, according to the person's behavior, activity, or attitude at that moment. According to the Kwakiutl, animals can supernaturally change their appearance at will and take on human form, and humans can transform into animals, birds, or fish. The Indians believe in the oneness of all of Earth's creatures, human and animal.

   "Transformation masks are created to be worn during ceremonies, dances, and presentations. They are both theatrical and psychological, concealing the wearer's identity and then substituting a new, assumed identity for an old one. The masks are specially designed to create the illusion of change. Some are very complicated and are operated by pulling strings or pushing levers to 'open' the mask and reveal the transformation inside."

3. Distribute the "Under My Mask—I Am Amazing" handout. Read through it with the students. Answer questions and provide explanations and details as needed.

   While students are working on their masks, be available to offer advice and assistance at each step. Encourage the flexible use of materials in creating the base for the mask. Molded clear plastic packaging material is excellent for building shapes, especially facial details. Plastic water or milk containers make good bases and are easily cut with scissors. The basic shapes are pieced together and held by masking tape, glue, or staples.

   Encourage elaborate detail and bold colors in keeping with the Kwakiutl Indian traditions. Recurring images are the raven, bear, whale, eagle, frog, and salmon.

4. Allow time for students to share their finished masks with the class, explaining the meaning and significance of the transformations. Evaluate the students' projects, or have students evaluate each other's projects. Ask the school librarian or media center director for space to display the students' transformation masks.

EXPERIENCE NOTES

Allow sufficient time for full exploration of this medium and subject matter. The culture of the Northwest Coast is rich in traditions and stories.

It is best if students start by planning their masks and drawing what they expect the finished products will look like. However, as is often the case in objects made with "found" or recycled materials, the materials themselves affect the outcome, and a mask may change during production. The purpose of this project is not so much to follow a plan as it is to create an expressive object. Be willing to "let it happen," and don't insist that students stick to their plans.

Expanding on the Project

- If possible, show one or more documentary films on the Native Americans of the Northwest Coast, or visit a nearby museum that has a Native American exhibit. For help finding videos to purchase, call Video Trackers, 1-800-718-4336, or Video Finders, 1-800-343-4727.

- Have the students wear their finished masks as they tell some of the wonderful tales and legends of the Native Americans of the Northwest Coast.

- Read aloud the poem, "Listen, Please Hear What I'm Not Saying," by Stephen Joseph.

- Have the students read *I Heard the Owl Call My Name*, a novel by Margaret Craven set in a Northwest Coast Indian village.

Alternative Projects

- Mask-making can be a fascinating unit of study for any age group. It can serve as an introduction to almost any culture in the world, as most countries and civilizations use masks in one way or another. For multidisciplinary thematic teaching, masks are an excellent, broad theme.

- The Native Americans of the Northwest Coast created elaborate totem poles that told the history of a family or their exploits with a supernatural being. Students could draw their own totems or build models using cardboard tubes as a base, telling their own family histories.

Resources

Craven, Margaret. *I Heard The Owl Call My Name.* (New York: Dell Publishing Company, 1980.) Also available: *I Heard the Owl Call My Name—Study Guide* by Patricia A. Halverson. (New Hyde Park, NY: Learning Links Inc., 1993.)

Sivin, Carole. *Maskmaking.* (Worcester, MA: Davis Publications, Inc., 1986.)

Most libraries have ample materials available on Indian cultures and arts. Suggestions:

— Bierhorst, John. *The Mythology of North America.* (New York: William Morrow and Company, 1985.) See especially Part I: "Northwest Coast," pages 25–53.

— Carlson, Laurie. *More than Moccasins: A Kid's Activity Guide to Traditional North American Indian Life.* (Chicago: Chicago Review Press, 1994.) More than 100 illustrated crafts and activities encourage students to explore Native American life and values. Written for ages 3–9, this is still a good resource for the upper elementary and middle school classroom.

— *Joseph Campbell and the Power of Myth with Bill Moyers.* This six-part video series is a fascinating tour of comparative mythology. Check your local library or video rental store. The series is also available on audio cassette.

— Campbell, Joseph. *The Power of Myth.* (New York: Doubleday, 1991.) The companion book to the video and audio series.

— Stewart, Hilary. *Looking at Indian Art of the Northwest Coast.* (Seattle, WA: University of Washington Press, 1979.)

Under My Mask

I Am Amazing

You have the power to change your face at will. Your outer face conceals the "real you," which you are about to reveal in a transformation mask of your own design.

1 Start by brainstorming a list of ideas for your personal transformation mask. Use these questions to guide your thinking:

- What transformations have you experienced in your life? (Think broadly. Go beyond the obvious transformations of growing up. Have you changed your attitudes? Your thinking? Your likes and dislikes? Your interests? Your friends? What else?)

- What transformations are you going through right now?

- What transformations do you anticipate experiencing in the future?

- What happens when you undergo a transformation? How does it feel? If other people could see a transformation in your face, what would they see?

- If you could transform into something else, what would it be?

- Can you think of shapes that might represent the transformations in your life?

- Can you think of colors that might represent the transformations?

Under My Mask

2 Draw or sketch a plan for your mask. Your mask will have three pieces, as shown in the illustration. It will also have two *finished* sides. Perhaps one side can show the outer you, and the other can show the inner you—the side you don't often reveal. Or one side can show the "you" of today, and the other can show a "you" that is yet to be.

Most masks will require three basic parts that will be connected loosely to allow for movement and transformation. As you sketch your mask, figure out the mechanics. Will you connect the parts with tape, string, staples, paper fasteners, rubber bands, or some combination? Make sure that the mechanics don't cover up or interfere with parts of your design.

FASTENERS/ HINGES GO HERE

3 Create the base for your mask, using any available materials you choose. Don't connect the parts yet.

4 If you *are not* going to cover your mask with papier-mâché, decorate it now. Paint the parts with one or two base colors. Sketch in your designs and details before adding more colors. Add small objects for elaboration, if desired.

5 If you *are* going to cover your mask with papier-mâché, make the mixture now. Cover each part of your mask with two layers of papier-mâché. Allow for holes, strings, or levers. Let the mask dry completely between layers and after the final layer. Decorate your mask.

6 When your mask is completely dry, connect the parts. Adjust your mask to fit your face.

SAIL AWAY WITH ME

The current trend in the travel industry is "theme vacations" geared to an individual's specific interest or hobby. There are chocolate tours of Europe, visits to famous authors' homes, "eco-tours" of pristine natural environments, adventure tours, and trips that take in museums around the world. One of the most popular venues for "theme travel" is a cruise ship. This project gives students the opportunity to design their own "Love Boat" experience.

Role Performance

Students design a cruise ship and plan a vacation.

Related Curriculum

Language Arts, Math, Art

Learning Objectives

By the end of this project, students will be able to:

- design and draw a cruise ship
- create a cruise line name, logo, and advertising campaign
- create a brochure describing their cruise and facilities
- plan a weekend of activities for passengers

Learning Styles

Affective, Cognitive, Individual, Cooperative

Materials Needed

- copies of the "Sail Away with Me: You'll Love My Boat" handout (pages 64–65) for each student
- cruise line and travel brochures
- magazines with photographs of cruise ships and ports of call
- large pieces of white drawing paper
- colored pencils and/or felt-tipped markers
- rulers
- scissors
- rubber cement or white glue

Doing the Project

1. Some students in your group may be seasoned travelers. Invite them to share their experiences with their classmates, especially if they include cruises. Ask them to relate their "best and worst" cruise ship moments, and to describe the ship(s) in as much detail as they can remember. Then introduce the project by announcing that everyone will have the chance to take an imaginary cruise on a ship of their own design.

2. Distribute the "Sail Away with Me: You'll Love My Boat" handout. Read through it with the students. Answer questions and provide explanations and details as needed.

   While students are working, let them browse through the cruise line and travel brochures you have collected. Be available to offer advice and assistance at each step. Students may need special help preparing their brochures. You may want to choose an especially good example, then go over it with the group as a whole. Point out headlines, descriptive language, and details. Look for details they might want to include in their own ship designs.

3. When the students are finished with their brochures, set up a table to display them. Designate a few "travel agents" to sit at the table, and have students sign up for their favorite cruises. When a student "books" a cruise, the "agent" issues a boarding pass and gives the tear-off stub to the originator of the cruise.

4. Evaluate the students' projects, or have students evaluate each other's projects, perhaps awarding extra honors to the most popular cruises.

EXPERIENCE NOTES

Most students' ideas of cruises and cruise ships come from television programs and movies. My students had a hard time grasping the concept of how *large* cruise ships really are. You might communicate this by describing a cruise ship as a "floating city," with almost every imaginable service and facility available.

Expanding on the Project

■ Students could design "theme cruises" for famous people in history or today's celebrities. For example, a scientific cruise for Ben Franklin would include "Kitchen Chemistry" cooking classes, a laser-light show, kite flying on deck (rain or shine), and perhaps a reunion of the Founding Fathers. This could be a fun research project if you supply a list of interesting personalities—or perhaps let students choose their own.

Alternative Projects

■ Vary the activity and let students design an aircraft, a train (steam locomotive? high-speed train?), or a spacecraft. (You may want to offer this alternative to anyone who is prone to seasickness!)

■ Have students compare today's cruise ships with famous (and infamous) cruise ships and luxury liners from history, perhaps including the *Titanic.*

Resources

Many travel agencies are happy to give travel brochures to teachers for use in the classroom. You can also obtain brochures by writing directly to cruise lines. Examples:

—Carnival Cruise Line, 3655 NW 87 Avenue, Miami, FL 33178

—Cunard Line, 555 Fifth Avenue, New York, NY 10017

—Princess Cruise Lines, 10100 Santa Monica Blvd., Los Angeles, CA 90067; 1-800-421-1700

—Royal Cruise Line, 1 Maritime Plaza, San Francisco, CA 94111

Request a sample issue of *Cruise Travel* magazine. Write or call: Cruise Travel Magazine, 990 Grove St., Evanston, IL 60201; (708) 491-6440.

Cruising season is March through May. Most travel magazines feature articles on cruises in their winter issues (January–February). See, for example, *Travel and Leisure.*

If you're a member of the AAA auto club, check their monthly magazine, *Car and Travel,* for information on cruises. You can also call their office to request pamphlets and brochures. (If you're not a member of AAA, you probably know someone who is.)

Old travel magazines are great sources of photographs for the students' brochures. See if local professional offices (doctors, dentists) have any they are willing to let you have.

Biesty, Stephen. *Stephen Biesty's Incredible Cross-Sections.* (New York: Alfred A. Knopf Books for Young Readers, 1992.) One of the meticulously detailed cross-sections in this book depicts the *Queen Mary* ocean liner.

SAIL AWAY WITH ME

You'll Love My Boat

Let others have their hotel chains, sports teams, and designer perfumes! You own a cruise line and you're about to launch a new ship in honor of yourself. The theme of the first cruise will be a celebration of you. Everything about the ship will reflect your personality, interests, abilities, hobbies, and preferences. All of the events will be things you like to do. The passengers will be surrounded by your favorite colors, foods, activities, entertainment, and performers. The gift shops will be filled with your personal selections. Ports of call will be places you want to visit and explore. This is your ultimate "fantasy cruise"!

1 Study cruise line brochures, pictures of cruise ships, articles about cruise ships . . . anything you can find. Then design your own cruise ship. Make a detailed drawing that shows a cross-section or aerial view. Designate specific accommodations and public areas.

2 Give your cruise line a name. Give your ship a name.

3 Design a color logo to represent your cruise line. It should be at least 2" x 3".

Sail Away with Me

4 Create a slogan or jingle to be used in an advertising campaign for your new cruise ship.

5 Make a brochure that describes the first cruise—the one that celebrates you. The cruise will last a weekend, from Friday evening through Sunday evening. Your brochure will be a "tri-fold" piece of paper or booklet that includes information on the following:

- how the staterooms (private rooms) are decorated (traditional, contemporary, historic, or . . . ?)
- the entertainment available on the ship, and descriptions of the facilities
- a schedule of day and evening events (read-a-thons? dueling guitars?)
- exercise and sports opportunities and facilities (bingo? in-line skating? swimming? aerobics?)
- celebrity guests (who will sit at the Captain's table with you?)
- appropriate style(s) of dress (casual during the day, formal at dinner? or casual all day?)
- the ports you will visit
- any sightseeing you will do.

Start by preparing a rough draft of the text. Proofread each other's brochures. If you have access to a computer, you may want to prepare your final copy on the computer. Remember to write or set your copy in columns.

6 Design a boarding pass with a tear-off stub at the bottom. Include your cruise line logo and ship name on both parts; leave space for the passenger's name and booking dates. Make several copies.

MEOPOLY

Everyone who has ever played board games has a favorite, one that evokes strong memories of fun, learning, or a special challenge. This project guides students through the process of creating their own board games using themselves as the theme. When complete, each game will be an unusual self-portrait or "autobiography."

Role Performance

Students invent a board game.

Related Curriculum

Language Arts, Math, Art

Learning Objectives

By the end of this project, students will be able to:
- use critical thinking skills to analyze games
- brainstorm ideas
- create and follow a plan
- exhibit improved crafts skills

Learning Styles

Affective, Cognitive, Individual

Materials Needed

- copies of the "Meopoly: A Very Personal Board Game" handout (pages 69–72) for each student
- large pieces of paper, cut into 15" squares (for planning)
- pencils and erasers
- rulers and yardsticks
- carbon paper
- large paper clips, masking tape, straight pins, paper fasteners, rubber cement or white glue
- illustration board, foam core, or thin wood, cut into 15" squares
- ballpoint pens in at least 2 colors
- scissors
- permanent colored markers (or acrylic paints and small brushes)
- stick-on vinyl letters or stencils for game titles
- miscellaneous materials for game pieces (foam core scraps, pieces of wood, plasticene clay, old game pieces, plastic bottle caps, etc.)
- construction paper for game cards
- clear contact paper for game cards, or a laminating machine
- resealable plastic bags or boxes for storing games and game pieces

Doing the Project

1. A few days before beginning this project, ask the students to bring in their favorite board games—those they play now or loved when they were younger. Have your favorites on hand, too.

2. Introduce the project with a class discussion about the various games. Ask questions like the following for each game (or as many as time allows):

   ◗ What makes this a good game?

   ◗ Why is it so popular?

   ◗ Is this game a classic? How many generations have played it?

   ◗ What's the object of the game?

   ◗ How are the rules explained? Are they easy to understand and follow? Are they complicated?

   ◗ Is the game easy to learn and play?

   ◗ Are there any special challenges?

   ◗ Is the game different enough each time you play it to keep you interested?

   ◗ What are the game pieces?

   ◗ How are the game cards designed? Are they easy to read and understand? Which cards do all players hope they get, and why?

   ◗ What determines a player's turn? Dice? A spinner? Cards?

   ◗ How is the game packaged?

   ◗ How many colors are used in the game? How many shapes?

   ◗ What makes the lettering or logo style right for this game?

3. Distribute the "Meopoly: A Very Personal Board Game" handout. Read through it with the students. Answer questions and provide explanations and details as needed. While students are working on their board games, be available to offer advice and assistance at each step.

Emphasize the importance of making a well-crafted game. An attractive, clean, easy-to-understand game will be played, not hidden in a closet.

4. Schedule a few class periods for "game evaluation days." Have the students play the games, then evaluate each one. One way to evaluate the games is by using a rating scale of 1–10, with 1 being "very" and 10 being "not at all." Apply the scale to each of these criteria:

   ◗ how easy the game is to learn

   ◗ how much fun it is to play

   ◗ how well the various elements (game board, pieces, cards, etc.) go together

   ◗ how well-crafted it is

   ◗ how clear the rules are

   ◗ how well it is designed

   ◗ how well it is packaged

   ◗ how well it reflects the person who created it.

   Total the points for each game, then announce the winner.

Experience Notes

Making personal board games works well as a culminating activity for the year. Planning and organization skills are essential for success, and these skills may not be present (or as strong) in the fall. On the other hand, I have found this project to be a good motivator for students who need to improve their planning and organization skills.

Many of my students win awards for their finished games at the county youth fair. Their smiles are worth the time and effort this project takes.

Expanding on the Project

■ Once students understand the process of making board games, this can easily be applied to other content areas to reinforce learning. Encourage students to use alternatives to the standard question-and-answer format, especially if the other players don't know as much about the subject. (It's no fun to play a game that tests knowledge you don't have.)

■ As a follow-up activity, have students create advertisements or commercials for their games.

Alternative Projects

■ Have students invent their games in cooperative learning groups.

■ Have students invent cooperative games rather than competitive games. In a cooperative game, the fun is in the playing, not in keeping score. There is no clear "winner," and all players feel good about themselves during and after the game. To learn more about cooperative games, read *The Cooperative Sports & Games Book*, *The Second Cooperative Sports & Games Book*, and *Playfair: Everybody's Guide to Non-Competitive Play*.

■ Make this a lesson in recycling and renewal. Collect old board games, with missing pieces and broken boxes. (Find them at garage sales, yard sales, tag sales, estate sales, charity resale stores . . . or in the backs of students' closets.) Have students mix-and-match parts and repair boxes to create brand-new games. Encourage them to alter the boards using paints and other materials.

Resources

Moberg, Randy. *TNT Teaching: Over 200 Dynamite Ways to Make Your Classroom Come Alive.* (Minneapolis: Free Spirit Publishing Inc., 1994). See especially the "Design-a-Game Kit" on pages 137–146.

Orlick, Terry. *The Cooperative Sports & Games Book: Challenge without Competition.* (New York: Pantheon Books, 1978.)

Orlick, Terry. *The Second Cooperative Sports & Games Book: Over 200 Brand-New Noncompetitive Games for Kids and Adults Both.* (New York: Pantheon Books, 1982.)

Winstein, Matt, and Joel Goodman. *Playfair: Everybody's Guide to Non-Competitive Play.* (San Luis Obispo, CA: Impact Publishers Inc., 1980.)

World Wide Games, P.O. Box 513, Colchester, CT 06415; 1-800-243-9232. Request a catalog from this distributor of handcrafted games, including many from different cultures and countries.

MEOPOLY

A Very Personal Board Game

Think for a moment about your favorite board game. You know every detail on the board by heart, and you could explain the game to anyone. You could describe the parts easily and even give advice about how to win.

The game that has brought you so many hours of fun began with many hours of hard work and planning. You're about to create your own board game, which will also take some hard work and planning. When you're through, you'll have a game you'll never get tired of playing . . . because it's about *you*.

Step 1: Brainstorming

Start by brainstorming words and phrases about you and your life. Use the categories listed here. Write your words and phrases on paper.

your birthplace or hometown

places you've lived

your interests

your hobbies

schools you've attended

your honors and awards

vacations you've taken

your family

your likes

your favorite subjects

your talents

your greatest achievements

your favorite music

your dreams and goals

your pets

your favorite colors

your dislikes

your best memories

your skills

other categories of your choosing

summer camps you've attended

your biggest challenges

MEOPOLY

Step 2: Planning

When you have completed your list, think about how these categories and responses could be included as parts of a board game about you. You could use a traditional board game design or come up with something very imaginative of your own.

Step 3: Decision-Making

Decide how your game will be played. Consider these questions and outline your answers:

- What will be the object of the game?
- Will there be questions to answer?
- Does a player have to get to a certain spot on the board in order to win? How is that accomplished?
- Will the game have penalties, rewards, challenges, or opportunities for players?
- Will there be places to visit, secrets to uncover, or problems to solve?

Step 4: Naming

What will you call your game? Brainstorm a list of possibilities. Sketch the lettering and some decorations. Does your name say what you want it to say? Does it look how you want it to look?

Step 5: Drawing

You'll need a pencil, an eraser, a large piece of paper (the exact size of your game board), and a ruler or yardstick to draw the layout of your game board. Be open to making many changes along the way (that's why you need an eraser). Draw or measure out the spaces and general design. This paper will become your master plan. Make sure it looks exactly the way you want it to before you go on to the next step. If you are using words, check that they are legible and spelled correctly.

Step 6: Transferring Your Design

Tape four pieces of carbon paper together, applying the tape to the non-carbon side. Secure this to your game board, carbon side down, using straight pins or paper clips. Place your paper plan on top of the carbon paper and secure it to the board as well.

Trace over all of your lines and words with a different color ballpoint pen. (For example, if you drew your layout in black pencil, use red pen to trace it. Then it will be easy to see which lines you have traced.) The pressure of your tracing will leave a carbon impression on the board, giving you an exact duplicate of your design. Remove the carbon paper and paper plan before going on to the next step.

Step 7: Adding Color

Color is very important in board game design, but be careful not to overdo it. Choose no more than four colors. If you use yellow for lettering, outline each letter in black. The whole board will look best if shapes are outlined with a thin, black, permanent marker.

Step 8: Making Tokens and Game Pieces

You will need at least four "tokens" or games pieces. These should relate to the theme of your game—you and your life. For example, if you are an athlete, your tokens could be symbols of sports equipment. If you are an animal lover, you might use miniature replicas of your pets. If you are a musician, try small instruments or symbols from music. Or your tokens can represent a variety of interests, talents, and skills.

Tokens should be small, detailed, and made from material that won't fall apart when handled. Baked plasticene clay, old toy parts combined to create new ones, foam core, and wood all work well.

MEOPOLY

Step 9: Making Game Cards

Type your words, sentences, questions, clues, etc. on paper, using a typewriter or a computer. Leave plenty of space between individual "cards." Check spelling and meaning. Carefully cut out the "cards," and use rubber cement to glue the pieces onto construction paper shapes. Laminate them (if a laminating machine is available) or cover them with clear contact paper.

Step 10: Making a Spinner

If your game requires a spinner, use a small piece of illustration board for a base. Decorate it and add numbers, words, symbols, or whatever matches your game board. Cut out an arrow from another piece of board. Poke a hole in the arrow and attach it to the spinner with a brass paper fastener.

Step 11: Writing the Rules

Study the written rules of other board games you enjoy to get an idea of how to write your own rules. Type your rules on paper, using a typewriter or a computer. Begin by explaining the object of the game and how players win. Ask a friend to read through your rules. Are they easy to understand?

Step 12: Packaging Your Game

Design a box or cover for your game when it's complete. You can cut your board in half, make fabric hinges on the back so it can fold, then put it in a box or cloth cover. Put the name of your game on the board and on any packaging. Place your game pieces and cards in a resealable plastic bag or a small decorated box.

When your masterpiece is finished, sign your name in the corner and write the date. Now you're ready to play! Find some friends and try your game. Play it with your family. How do people respond to your game? Is it challenging? Fun? Do they want to play it again . . . and again?

WHAT'S MY LINE?

How connected are we to each other, and what can we learn from lines? This project gives students the freedom to explore materials, abstract ideas, and lines, first as individuals and then in small groups.

Role Performance

Students create, combine, and analyze lines.

Related Curriculum

Language Arts, Humanities, Art

Learning Objectives

By the end of this project, students will be able to:

▨ think abstractly about line

▨ examine various examples of line quality in art

▨ experiment with flexible use of materials

▨ evaluate line quality

▨ work cooperatively in a group

▨ participate in a group oral presentation

Learning Styles

Affective, Cognitive, Individual, Cooperative

Materials Needed

▨ copies of the handout, "What's My Line? It's My Design" (pages 76–77) for each student

▨ books, prints, and/or slides showing a variety of examples of art, preferably modern and abstract expressionism

▨ miscellaneous "junk" to use as painting implements, supplied by the students (see #1 in "Doing the Project")

▨ white construction paper cut into 4" x 6" pieces, 10 per student

▨ black tempera paint in various consistencies

▨ egg cartons or aluminum pie plates

▨ masking tape

▨ paint shirts or cover-ups

Doing the Project

1. One week before beginning this project, assign the following as homework: "Collect a small bag of assorted 'junk' such as plastic game parts, corks, string, rubber bands, cotton swabs, broken hair accessories, pencil erasers, springs, etc. and bring it to class." Explain nothing at this point. This adds to the mystery of "what's coming" and encourages creativity.

2. The day before beginning this project, assign this homework: "Bring in a line." Answer no questions about the assignment, then expect anything and everything. The results will be very surprising. You may see a line of poetry, a toy telephone line, a line of false compliments, a coiled wire, a line from a play, etc. Some students will bring in a straight line drawn on paper. Have each student share what they brought. Praise examples of flexible and creative thinking.

3. Introduce the project by showing reproductions of famous works of modern art. Call attention to the various qualities of line. Point out how thick, jagged lines seem to express anger, strong emotion, or determined movement. Find thin, wispy, or active lines that indicate other feelings or scattered motion. Elicit comments about how lines can create moods in patterns or designs. Pictures can seem to be "quiet" or "noisy," "calm" or "tense" because of line texture.

4. On Day 1 of the project:

   ▶ Cover the work space with newspaper.

   ▶ Set up the black tempera in egg cartons or aluminum pie plates to be shared in small groups.

   ▶ Give each student 10 pieces of 4" x 6" white construction paper. Have them write their names or initials on the back of each piece, in pencil.

   ▶ Explain that they are going to create lines on their papers with the black tempera. Instead of brushes, they will use the "junk" they

collected earlier. Each line must go from edge to edge horizontally across the paper, because it will eventually be matched up with other lines. The point is to create lines that express feeling and personality. Demonstrate a few examples.

5. On Day 2 of the project:

   ▶ Direct the students to gather all of their individual lines and begin to evaluate them, picking only four of their favorites. Students should look for the most interesting lines. Again, it is essential that the selected lines extend to both sides of the paper. Place all of the discards in a box for future use.

   ▶ Divide the class into small groups. Tell the students that they are to attempt to join all of their lines to create one long, continuous line. For best results, the individual segments should join "naturally" so that the final line seems to have a life of its own. Once they have arranged their segments, they can join the pieces with masking tape on the backs.

   ▶ Direct the small groups to create a story about their line's "life." Tell them that they will be presenting their story to the class as a group. Allow enough class time for the groups to prepare their stories.

6. On Day 3 of the project:

   ▶ Invite the groups to present their stories orally to the class.

   ▶ Evaluate the projects, or let the different groups evaluate each other's projects. They should consider the quality of the line, the story, and the presentation.

   ▶ Display the finished lines in the classroom. They are intriguing and graphically interesting when hung as a border around the room.

7. Distribute the "What's My Line? It's My Design" handout. Read through it with the students. Explain that the questions are meant to help them reflect on the project and what the experience meant to them personally. You might use this handout as a journal assignment.

EXPERIENCE NOTES

I have always found this project exciting to teach because of the students' enthusiastic response and the wonderfully expressive results. It's an art activity that guarantees success for each student.

In the affective realm, students discover truths about how individuals change as they relate to each other. They notice that some lines "fit in" easily while others don't fit in anywhere and need to be left alone. Some line segments that seemed "boring" are greatly enhanced when paired with someone else's line. Class discussions of this project become very abstract as students relate the lines to real life and to interactions between people.

Peer evaluation of this project can be creative, sensitive, and fun. If you decide to display the finished lines in a border around the room, you may find that students remember the stories for quite some time.

Expanding on the Project

- Perhaps while waiting for the paint to dry, share one or both of these wonderful read-aloud books with the students, *The Dot and the Line* and *The Missing Piece*.

- Connect the "lines" students bring to class and see what happens. (A string connected to a line of poetry connected to a telephone line connected to a line from a play connected to a "bottom line"? This offers interesting possibilities.)

Alternative Projects

- Have the students create *analog drawings* as metaphors for emotions or human characteristics. This activity, which teaches about the power and meaning of line, is fully discussed and accompanied by exact teaching instructions in Betty Edwards's book, *Drawing on the Artist Within*.

- Create class poems from favorite lines of poetry. Each student contributes 10 lines. Working in small groups, the students decide which lines to keep, which to discard, and how to order the lines. Have them title their poems and read them aloud to the class. Which poems work? What happens to the meaning of a well-known line when it is connected to lines from other poems?

Resources

Check your local library or media center for books, prints, and/or slides featuring the work of artists Franz Kline, Adolph Gottlieb, Arshile Gorky, Wassily Kandinsky, Ellsworth Kelly, Pablo Picasso, and others.

Edwards, Betty. *Drawing on the Artist Within: An Inspirational and Practical Guide to Increasing Your Creative Powers*. (New York: Simon & Schuster Trade Division, 1987), pages 66–74.

Juster, Norman. *The Dot and the Line*. (New York: Random House, 1977.) Also available as an 8mm film. Check with your district film library.

Silverstein, Shel. *The Missing Piece*. (New York: HarperCollins Children's Books, 1976.)

What's My Line?

It's My Design

If we take the time to reflect on the things we do, we often find that we have learned many things about ourselves in the process. The following questions invite you to reflect on the line activity you just completed. Answer the questions as honestly and as completely as you can. (Write your answers on a separate sheet of paper, or in your journal.) Express your true feelings.

1 What was your favorite part of this project? Why?

2 What was the most difficult part for you? Why?

3 What part of the project surprised you? Why?

4 Was it easy or difficult for you to select four lines out of the ten you made? Explain.

WHAT'S MY LINE?

5 Describe the way your group worked together to create one continuous line. Were there any disagreements? If so, how did you resolve them?

6 Who in your group assumed a leadership role? If you did, was this a new or different experience for you?

7 Describe the way your group worked together to create a story about your line. Is there anything you would add to that story now?

8 Have you ever felt like your emotions were moving and changing, like the rhythm of a line? Describe an experience you remember.

9 When trying to connect the lines, you might have found that some of them did not easily match up with others. Some of them seemed to be made for each other. Some looked better and worked best when they were connected to others. Some looked better and worked best when they were left alone. Some had to be moved around a lot before you found the right lines to connect them with. Some never fit in anywhere.

Do you think this project could be a metaphor for human experience? Explore this in a paragraph or two.

Personal Recipes

In the "kitchens of their minds," students create recipes for different moods and life experiences. This allows for the objective introspection of events, with space for humor as well as catharsis.

Role Performance

Students write a personal cookbook.

Related Curriculum

Language Arts, Math

Learning Objectives

By the end of this project, students will be able to:
- write "recipes" following the standard format
- exhibit improved sequential thinking
- use measurements for description
- create a personal cookbook

Learning Styles

Affective, Cognitive, Individual

Materials Needed

- copies of the "Personal Recipes: Measuring Memories" handout (pages 80–81) for each student
- a variety of cookbooks or food magazines for recipe examples
- a supply of 4" x 6" index cards

Doing the Project

1. Introduce the project by writing the following on the chalkboard or showing it on an overhead projector:

A Perfect Teaching Experience

1 well-prepared lesson
a roomful of eager students
10 good questions
a 20-minute discussion
appropriate equipment
a comfortable room temperature
interesting content
no interruptions
lots of positive feedback
a dash of humor
a sprinkle of creativity

Directions: Mix together with a smile. Serve in an interesting manner. Let information incubate. Review and reinforce the following day.

Let the recipe generate discussion. Invite the students to create a recipe, as a group, for the "perfect class" or "the perfect teacher." Put their responses on the board or the overhead projector.

2. Distribute the "Personal Recipes: Measuring Memories" handout. Read through it with the students. Answer questions and provide explanations and details as needed. While students are working on their recipes, be available to offer advice and assistance at each step.

The required amount of recipes will depend on the age and interest level of your group. Give students the option of writing their recipes by hand or preparing them on a typewriter or computer. They can be bound as a booklet or remain loose as recipe cards.

3. Evaluate the students' projects, or have students evaluate each other's projects. Which recipes would they like to try? Which seem especially interesting or "tasty"?

EXPERIENCE NOTES

This project gives students practice in focusing on details, sequencing information, and analyzing experiences. Some students may become blocked by the need to list things in order, so encourage "free brainstorming" first. Have students listen to and comment on each other's directions.

Expanding on the Project

- Have each student choose a recipe to try again in real life. Afterward, ask them to report on whether their recipes were successful. Did they have to change any of the ingredients? Which ones? How? Did they have to change any of the steps?

Alternative Projects

- Have students write "recipes for success." They can print them neatly on white paper, type them, or prepare them on a computer. Let them illustrate their recipes. Make copies for everyone or bind the recipes into a class handbook.

- Ask the students to bring in favorite family recipes. Create a class cookbook.

Resources

Fortunately, cookbooks and articles about cooking aren't hard to find. A few weeks before beginning this project, you might start clipping recipes out of the newspaper or saving articles from cooking magazines. Bring in a few of your favorite cookbooks. If any of your students enjoy cooking, they might bring in their favorite cookbooks or recipes. You simply want to make sure to have an abundance of examples available.

PERSONAL RECIPES

Measuring Memories

1 Sometimes we view our lives as a series of flashbacks to past experiences, events, and situations. Choose one or more of these to think about now:

a family vacation   a challenge you faced   a day at the beach   a problem you solved

a big mistake   a personal achievement   a birthday party   a personal crisis

a personal success   a difficult time in your life   a time when you felt proud

a perfect day at school   a day off   a time when you felt sad or disappointed   a happy day

a time when a friend supported you

a time when a friend let you down

a natural disaster in your town (flood, earthquake, tornado, hurricane)

Consider the different "ingredients" that were involved in each experience, event, or situation you are thinking about. Who else was there? What did they contribute? What was the environment like? What did *you* contribute? What were your feelings? If the experience was positive for you, what made it that way? If the experience was negative for you, what made it that way? If it started off negative but ended up positive, what changed things? Was it something you did, said, or thought?

Personal Recipes

2 Brainstorm a list of experiences, events, and situations from your life. These can be positive or negative, simple or complex, long ago or recent. (You can use some of the items from the list in #1, if you like.)

3 Create a recipe for one or more of the experiences, events, or situations you brainstormed in #2. List the ingredients that were necessary for each one to exist. Use measurements to indicate how much of each ingredient was present.

4 Once you have listed all of your ingredients, add the directions. Be clear and concise. Don't leave out anything important. Here's an example:

A Perfect Day at the Beach

1 bright sun	sunglasses
a cloudless sky	1 beach bag
3 close friends	2 new magazines
1 new bathing suit	1 portable CD player
1 big straw hat	5 favorite CD's
1 large beach towel	20 oz. of bottled water
a 10 oz. tube of sunscreen	a 20 oz. bag of chips

Directions: Check the weather forecast. Call three friends. Put on new bathing suit and sunscreen. Mix together remaining ingredients in beach bag. Find transportation for you and three friends. Do not overcook. Have fun!

Time Treasures

Stuff! We are overloaded with it—in our homes, our closets, and our classrooms. Yet how many times have we secretly said, "Oh, I wish I hadn't given (or thrown) that away"? Most families have someone who holds on to "stuff" for the grandchildren. In this activity, students predict what things they would like to hold on to for their grandchildren to see again sometime in the future.

Role Performance

Students assemble a personal time capsule.

Related Curriculum

Language Arts, Science, Social Studies, Art

Learning Objectives

By the end of this project, students will be able to:

- brainstorm a list of items
- collect or represent the items
- find or create a special container for the items
- write a detailed letter explaining their choices

Learning Styles

Affective, Cognitive, Individual

Materials Needed

- copies of the student handout, "Time Treasures: Wait Until You See This" handout (pages 84–85) for each student
- books and/or magazines about antiques and collecting
- containers for the items the students collect (students should provide their own containers)

Doing the Project

1. Introduce the project by bringing in "old stuff" of your own to share—an heirloom, a childhood toy or book, a favorite antique, and/or pictures of very old objects or mementos. If possible, borrow some antique toys.

2. Distribute the "Time Treasures: Wait Until You See This" handout. Read through it with the students. Answer questions and provide explanations and details as needed. (You may want to present the introductory paragraph as an imagination exercise.) While students are working on their collections, be available to offer advice and assistance at each step.

   Help students find a good balance in their selection of items to include. These should represent many areas in their lives, not just entertainment. Encourage them to choose items that represent their values, interests, talents, likes, etc. in the here and now. Students should include about 15 items—or more, depending on ability and age level. Have available a selection of books and/or magazines on antiques and collecting for students to page through while they work on their collections.

3. For evaluation purposes, a display and discussion would be revealing and informative. Have the students explain why they chose to include specific items in their time capsules. If students include very personal items, give them the option of not sharing those. During the discussion, you might ask the students to tell what they learned about each other from this project.

EXPERIENCE NOTES

During the course of this project, many students become curious about the teenage days of their parents, grandparents, and great-grandparents. This often initiates wonderful family dialogues. Interviewing older relatives would be a meaningful follow-up assignment or motivating activity; you may want to schedule this project close to a major holiday, when extended families get together.

This should be a project that students really want to keep for years to come.

Expanding on the Project

- Invite senior citizens to be guest speakers. Encourage them to bring "time treasures" (and memories) to share with the class. Have the students prepare questions in advance.

- Invite an antiques dealer to be a guest speaker. Ask him or her to bring old toys, books, mementos, and other collectibles and oddities to display and explain.

- You might include this project in a unit on the future. Students could "predict" the future, try to imagine what will be obsolete, and identify present-day items that will someday be "old treasures."

- Musically inclined students might enjoy compiling lists of songs that have time as a major theme, or include the word "time" in the title or lyrics. They could create audiocassette

recordings of parts of these songs to play on the day the time capsules are presented to the class.

Alternative Projects

- Ask the students to tape (video or audio) interviews with older relatives, neighbors, or family friends. They should prepare questions in advance. For ideas, consult William Zimmerman's book, *How to Tape Instant Oral Biographies*.

- Have the students write 2–3 page letters to themselves to be read in a month (or longer, depending on how much time remains in the school year). In their letters, they should describe what life is like for them in the here and now. What do they do on a typical day? What is important to them? Who are their friends? What are the big issues in their life? What are their goals, dreams, interests, likes, dislikes, talents, abilities, hopes, problems, etc.? How would they describe themselves? Provide envelopes and have students enclose their letters, seal the envelopes, and address them to themselves. Collect the envelopes. In a month (or on whatever "delivery date" you choose), hand the envelopes back to the students and have them read their letters (aloud or silently to themselves). Discuss as a class how things have changed for them within a relatively short time.

Resources

Zimmerman, William. *How to Tape Instant Oral Biographies*, 2nd edition. (New York: Guarionex Press, 1994.) Write to: Guarionex Press Ltd., 201 W. 77 Street, New York, NY 10024.

Check your local library for books and/or magazines on antiques and collecting. You'll probably find a wide variety, because people collect all kinds of things!

Time Treasures

Wait Until You See This!

Imagine that it is far in the future, and you are 85 years old. (Chances are you will reach that age and become a grandparent or great-grandparent someday.) Now imagine that you're spending an afternoon with your 13-year-old great-grandchild. You love each other, but you don't have much in common, and there's a gigantic generation gap between you. Conversation soon begins to lag, and you decide that it's the perfect moment to share something you made when you were a teenager (or almost a teenager). You walk to a closet, open it, dig deep in the back, and bring out a dusty container. Carefully, you carry it to where your great-grandchild is waiting. You explain that you've found a "time capsule" of you as an adolescent. You open it and begin to explore and discuss the contents—one item at a time, each one rich with memories . . . .

For this project, you will create a personal time capsule. Inside a container you make (or an existing container you embellish), you will place special items or things that represent those items. Perhaps you will keep your time capsule and share it in the faraway future.

What will you include in your time capsule? Each item must reflect you as you are today, in the here and now.

1 Ask yourself these questions and jot down answers on a separate sheet of paper:

* What am I all about?
* What are my likes? Dislikes? Hobbies? Skills? Dreams? Problems? Goals?
* How would I describe my school? Friends? Pets? Clothes? Favorite music? Favorite places? Favorite things to do? Other favorites?

2 Brainstorm a list of things that are important to you. These can be things you cherish, use daily, find essential, or just want to remember. What do you love now, today, that would be fun to rediscover in 70 years? Jot down ideas and descriptions.

Time Treasures

3 Using your notes from #1 and #2, make a list of items you would like to include in your time capsule. Add any other categories or items you choose.

4 For each item on your list, determine whether to put the item itself in your time capsule or use something else to represent it. For example, you probably won't want to put a watch in your time capsule. Instead, you might use a close-up photograph or a magazine advertisement. You probably can't include a costume you wore in a play, but you can include a sketch and perhaps a fabric sample. If you have a favorite computer game, you might use a printout of a screen from the game.

All items you include in your time capsule must be "time-safe." Use a clean wrapper from your favorite candy bar, not the candy itself. Newspaper yellows and deteriorates, so you may want to laminate any articles you want to include. Can you outwit technology? Perhaps laminated sheet music for your favorite song will outlast an audiocassette recording.

5 What kind of container will you use? Will you build one or redesign one that already exists? Do you have an heirloom container (such as a wooden box, a tin, or a hat box) that you received from an older relative? Consider size *and* durability. Your container will not be buried, but it should be able to withstand the passage of time. Cardboard is not a good choice.

Once you decide on a container, decorate it and perhaps give it a name. Make the outside interesting, attractive, even mysterious. It should inspire deep curiosity.

6 Write a letter to your future descendants. Describe each item in your time capsule, tell why it is important to you, and explain the context in which you used it. Date your letter. Include a recent photograph of yourself, either alone or with friends. (Be sure to write the date and the name of everyone pictured on the back.) Put your letter and photograph in an envelope, seal the envelope, and add it to your time capsule.

7 Your teacher might ask you to share your completed time capsule with the class. If you have included something very personal that you won't want to share, you may want to put it in a specially marked sealed envelope.

8 After you have shared your time capsule, take it home and store it in a safe place. Be sure to bring it with you when you leave home, go to college, move, etc. Then wait for the perfect moment to open it . . . perhaps in 70 years!

WE ARE WHAT WE WEAR

"How do I look?" That question is asked by millions of young people several times a day. The adolescent preoccupation with appearance is something we all went through, but most of us have forgotten what it really means: "Am I okay? Will I be accepted? I can't handle rejection." Or: "I'll show them. This is me. I need to be noticed. I need to express myself." Clothing is much more than "covering up" to a teen or a pre-teen.

For this project, students create descriptive clothing that represents who they are at this point in their lives. They express themselves through design and/or decoration. The project culminates in an oral presentation and "fashion show."

Role Performance

Students design and create outfits to wear.

Related Curriculum

Language Arts, Math, Art, Humanities

Learning Objectives

By the end of this project, students will be able to:

- use a variety of materials creatively and flexibly
- show originality and skill in elaboration
- show attention to detail
- explain the meanings behind their creations

Learning Styles

Affective, Cognitive, Individual

Materials Needed

- copies of the "We Are What We Wear: I Express Myself" handout (pages 89–90) for each student
- paper and pencils for sketching designs
- basic clothing components (plain T-shirts, jeans, dresses, skirts, jackets, hats; students should provide their own components)
- fabric or acrylic paints and brushes
- permanent markers
- tacky glue (for fabrics); hot glue guns
- needles and spools of thread
- scissors
- fabrics and decorative materials (students should provide supplies for their personal use and also, when possible, to share)
- cardboard
- wire hangers for works in progress

Doing the Project

1. Introduce the project by telling the students that they are going to make very personal "fashion statements." Use questions like the following to begin a discussion, or have students write responses in their journals.

   ▶ What is one favorite article of clothing you remember from when you were a child?

      —What did you love about it?

      —How did wearing it make you feel?

      —Did people ever comment about it?

      —What specific details about it can you recall?

   ▶ Have you saved any articles of clothing that no longer fit you? Why did you save those particular items? (For sentimental reasons? Because they remind you of a certain time, place, occasion, event, or person? Because they help you to remember a special occasion in your life?)

   ▶ Did you ever feel sad about outgrowing a favorite article of clothing? What happened to it? Did you hand it down to a younger sibling? Did you give it away? Did you donate it to a charitable organization? How did you feel about that?

   ▶ Did you ever wear a particular item of clothing so much that you finally wore it out?

   ▶ Think of a favorite article of clothing you own today—maybe you're wearing it right now.

      —Why do you like it so much?

      —What does it say about you?

2. Distribute the "We Are What We Wear: I Express Myself" handout. Read through it with the students. Answer questions and provide explanations and details as needed. While students are working on their outfits, be available to offer advice and assistance at each step.

Encourage students to be flexible and creative in choosing fabrics. Suggest burlap, natural materials, leaves, twigs, newsprint, muslin, twisted pieces of magazine pages, bubble wrap, etc. Supply cardboard for use between layers of fabric or clothing while painting or gluing.

Create a "central supply" area for decorative materials. Have plastic containers or boxes available for storing fabric pieces, ribbons, fancy papers, string, buttons, yarn, small "found" objects, etc. Encourage sharing. If the entire project is done in class, access to a sewing machine would be helpful.

3. Evaluate the students' projects, or have students evaluate each other's projects. They might award points for creativity, originality, the flexible use of materials, and "surprise" value, as well as how accurately the outfit represents the wearer. Consider holding a "fashion show" for another class or an all-school function.

Experience Notes

One of my students expressed herself best through painting and poetry, so she elected to sew a full skirt and top out of unbleached muslin, painted landscapes on it to represent her environmental concerns, then added original poetry with permanent markers.

Display day is always fun and exciting for everyone!

Expanding on the Project

- Divide the class into small groups. Have them research the subject of clothing, with special emphasis on finding new or enlightening information. For example, they might discover the beginnings of an article of clothing, a fabric, a fashion fad, or a designer. What about ceremonial clothing? Religious vestments? Undergarments? Traditions? How do fashions begin? What does it take to change a custom? Encourage the students to find out something obscure or esoteric about the fashion world. Instruct them to take notes on index cards and be ready to share their discoveries in a class discussion or presentation. Allow time for library visits or class periods spent in the media center.

- Students might enjoy surveying older relatives and others about the fashion "rebels" of their day. What clothing "statements" do people remember? What did they wear to express themselves?

- Create a display of photos from fashion magazines, with students' written comments about changing fashions and attitudes. Have students make comparisons with today's fashion trends.

- Invite a fashion designer (professional or student) to visit your class as a guest speaker. He or she might bring in sketches and examples to share with the class. Have the students prepare questions in advance.

Alternative Projects

- This project can be done more simply and on a smaller scale. Or have the students do it all on paper, making detailed drawings.

- Provide a generous supply of fashion magazines and have students create photo collages showing clothing that reflects their personalities. They might write "Why This Is Me" paragraphs to accompany their collages.

Resources

Boucher, François. *20,000 Years of Fashion: The History of Costume and Personal Adornment.* (New York: Harry N. Abrams, Inc., 1987.) A truly comprehensive, large format book—and expensive. Your best bet is to check a city library.

Peacock, John. *The Chronicle of Western Fashion from Ancient Times to the Present Day.* (New York: Harry N. Abrams, Inc., 1991.) Fully illustrated; an excellent resource.

WE ARE WHAT WE WEAR

I Express Myself

Imagine this situation: The alarm goes off. You drag yourself out of bed, wash up, and face your first problem-solving situation of the day: what to wear. (Sound familiar so far? Read on!) This is a special challenge, because there is no such thing as "ready-to-wear" clothing. There are no clothing stores or catalogs. Instead, the laws of your city, state, or country require each person to create his or her own clothing. By law, each outfit must be unique and representative of the wearer. In other words, what you put on today must say to the world, "This expresses me—my style, personality, individuality, hopes, fears, talents, dreams, favorites, etc." Anyone who sees you will understand who you are by looking at the clothes you are wearing.

Follow these steps to create your unique and representative outfit—a fashion statement of who you are at this point in your life.

1 Brainstorm a list of characteristics, traits, preferences, passions, talents, etc. that make you *you*—one of a kind.

2 Create a "personal basics" list of the clothes, fabrics, colors, and styles you most like to wear. For example, if you prefer denim pants, zippered cotton sweatshirts, and floppy hats, your list might look like this:

> sweatshirts (with zippers)
> hats (floppy)
> pants
> denim
> cotton

WE ARE WHAT WE WEAR

3 Next to each item on your "personal basics" list, jot down some unique and creative ways to enhance or personalize each one. Be original! For example, next to "pants" on your list, you might write:

cut off legs below knee, let edges fray, paint the pockets, sew on patches, glue on labels from soup cans, replace ordinary button at top with special button

4 Evaluate your ideas, then select your favorites. Elaborate on those. Start planning your personal fashion statement. Ask yourself these questions:

- What materials and supplies will I need?
- What articles of clothing will I bring from home? A plain T-shirt, pants, dress, or skirt? (Or will I start from scratch and create my own T-shirt, pants, or skirt?)
- What decorations will I bring to class? Will I have any to share?
- What will I want my outfit to say?

5 Create your outfit. Have fun making it . . . and wearing it!

BE CREATIVE, BUT BE TRUE TO YOUR IDEAS. IF YOUR FEELINGS ARE TRANSPARENT, PERHAPS CLEAR PLASTIC BUBBLE WRAP IS REALLY YOUR STYLE!

Bookself-Bookshelf

It's no secret that you can tell a lot about a person just by looking at his or her bookshelves. For this project, students will create an imaginary bookshelf that expresses the self, both in the style and design of the shelf and in the books displayed there. By the end of the project, they will all know each other a little better than before.

Role Performance

Students create a model of a bookshelf complete with books.

Related Curriculum

Language Arts, Art, Math

Learning Objectives

By the end of this project, students will be able to:

- brainstorm titles for books (real and imaginary) that are personally relevant to them
- incorporate design ideas into a personal metaphor
- plan a library display and make a model
- recall the Dewey Decimal System

Learning Styles

Affective, Cognitive, Individual

Materials Needed

- copies of the "Bookself-Bookshelf: Everybody Is a Book" handout (pages 94–95) for each student
- photographs or slides of bookshelf sections from a variety of libraries, public and personal
- assorted model-building materials including foam core, balsa wood, box lids, corrugated cardboard, plain cardboard, etc.
- scissors, X-acto knives (mat knives), paper cutter
- rulers, yardsticks
- rubber cement, white glue
- paints (tempera and/or acrylic), brushes, fine-line felt-tipped colored markers, colored pencils
- large pieces of white drawing paper
- assorted materials for details: gold or silver braid or cord saved from gifts; gold or silver markers; vinyl stick-on letters; etc.
- small pieces of sponge or foam (for 3-D effect)
- a chart showing the Dewey Decimal system (check your school media center or library)

Doing the Project

1. If possible, introduce this project to your students while sitting in a quiet corner of the school media center or library. This will set the mood and inspire them. Show photographs or slides of bookshelf sections from interesting libraries, friends' personal collections, or bookstores, especially small, independent bookstores. Try to reflect the variety of storage and display styles as well as book selections. While institutional libraries may be standardized, stress how one's own bookshelf can be a form of personal expression.

   During this introductory session, just try to impart your love of books and the importance of libraries. Encourage discussion about books in general: buying vs. borrowing, favorite books, favorite libraries, Presidential libraries, etc. Review the Dewey Decimal system, then give students time to browse and check out books for pleasure.

2. Begin the second session with a brief imagination exercise. Have the students sit comfortably, close their eyes, take a few deep breaths, and relax as you read the following. Pause between sentences.

   "You've just entered the most enormous, magnificent bookstore ever built. Everything is brand new and carefully organized. You notice that your favorite quiet music is playing as a smiling person hands you a large, empty basket with handles. You're invited to select any books that interest you because you're such a special human being. There are no limits or restrictions. You begin to walk down the aisles, scanning the shelves, pausing to read titles. You reach for certain books and page through them. Slowly you fill your basket with books of all sizes and colors."

   Let the students enjoy this experience for a few minutes, then ask them to gently open their eyes. Invite them to talk about how they felt during the exercise. Did most of them fill their baskets to the top? Were they looking forward to reading their books?

3. Distribute the "Bookself-Bookshelf: Everybody Is a Book" handout. Read through it with the students. Answer questions and provide explanations and details as needed. While students are working on their bookshelves, be available to offer advice and assistance at each step.

4. Evaluate the students' projects. Look for creativity, imagination, effort, variety, and evidence of the self. Afterward, arrange to show off your students' projects. Most librarians would welcome a display of completed projects, especially during National Library Week, which begins on the third Sunday of April.

EXPERIENCE NOTES

Students who have difficulty with small motor skills can create models on a larger scale. Mechanically-minded students may want to create a revolving bookshelf, or one with a hidden compartment.

Some students who are not avid readers may prefer to add "knick-knacks" that express an interest. Encourage them to focus on books, staying with the project's intent.

Expanding on the Project

- Ask students to create bookshelf plans for famous characters from history, today's news, or fiction. For example, what would Waldo (from *Where's Waldo?*), Superman, Maya Angelou, Steven Spielberg, Queen Elizabeth, Snoopy, Vincent van Gogh, Whitney Houston, Denzel Washington, Yo-Yo Ma, Gloria Estefan, Gary Larson, General Colin Powell, Bill Cosby, or the President of the United States have in their personal libraries?

- Some students may want to create a diorama of the room where their personal bookshelf would be.

Alternative Projects

* Instead of making a model, students could create large drawings or paintings of their bookshelves, showing the spines of the books (with titles). The two-dimensional format could also be done on a computer using a simple desktop publishing system.

* For a creative math challenge, have students invent a new system for classifying books. They might start by researching Melvil Dewey (1851–1931), who developed the system that was named after him, and by learning about the Library of Congress system.

Resources

Interior design magazines usually contain many photographs of bookshelves and bookcases. Ask librarians for soon-to-be-discarded magazines. Outdated catalogs from book publishers are other good sources of ideas.

For expert advice on dioramas, contact New York artist Jane Freeman. She creates miniature dioramas and writes a column about miniatures for *Nutshell News*. Write to: Jane Freeman, 21 Harrison Street, #3, New York, NY 10013. Be sure to include a self-addressed, stamped envelope. If you would like to receive a set of 12 full-color postcards of miniature dioramas, please include $5, which also covers postage.

BOOKSELF-BOOKSHELF

Everybody Is a Book

Can you believe it? The Library of Congress in Washington, D.C., has created a new category for classifying books. Libraries everywhere will use this category to create a section of books about you! You have been asked to create the criteria for book selection and display. To do this, you will make a model of a personal bookshelf filled with books of your choice. The books can be real or imaginary, but they all must reflect *who you are*.

1 Brainstorm a list of books you would include on your bookshelf. List any fiction and/or nonfiction books you feel would help people to understand who you are. These books do not really have to exist; perhaps they'll be written someday. (Maybe you'll write them yourself!) Make up some of the titles and authors. You may even want to include bound volumes of magazines.

2 Your valuable collection deserves a very special bookshelf which should also communicate something about you. For example, if you are a risk-taker, your shelf should also "take risks," maybe with a radical new design. If you are traditional, you might design a traditional bookshelf. Put aside your ideas of how bookshelves "should" look and see what happens.

Draw your design on paper, using markers, colored pencils, and rulers. You will need to make decisions about size, shape, color, appearance, material, cost, style, condition, lighting, supports, etc. Be precise and include as many details as possible. You will follow your design to build a scale model of your bookshelf. Use flexible thinking, but try to stay within 12"–18" for height.

Bookself-Bookshelf

3 Build your model from available materials—foam core, wood, box lids, cardboard, etc. The materials you use will determine how you will paint your model. Tempera will cause some curling on paper or foam core. Acrylic paint is best for wood and plastic.

USE A BOX
OR CRATE BASE

CUT FAKE BOOKS OUT
OF FOAM CORE

4 Once your model is painted (and the paint has dried), elaborate on it. You may want to create little books with titles and authors' names. (Refer to the list you brainstormed for #1 above.) You may want to add interesting objects or bookends. What choices will you make? How will you craft your books, objects, and/or bookends?

You might design and print your book labels on the computer, then cut and paste them on the book "spines." Photos (to scale) from magazines can be cut and pasted as well. For a 3-D effect, back some items with a tiny piece of sponge or foam before gluing. This becomes an exercise in making miniatures.

5 When your bookshelf is complete, ask yourself: "What secrets does this reveal about me and my world?" Have a friend look at your bookshelf, then tell you what it says about you. Did your friend learn anything new or surprising by studying your bookshelf?

Superhero

Students enjoy imagining themselves as superheroes/heroines. For this project, they create trading cards that picture the heroes/heroines they are now and the imaginary heroes/heroines they love to read about.

Role Performance

Students create trading cards.

Related Curriculum

Language Arts, Social Studies, Art

Learning Objectives

By the end of this project, students will be able to:

- appreciate their own uniqueness
- think objectively and imaginatively
- communicate ideas effectively
- exhibit crafts skills
- show improvement in the areas of originality and elaboration

Learning Styles

Affective, Individual

Materials Needed

- copies of the "Superhero? That's Me" handout (pages 98–99) for each student
- sample trading cards
- poster board in light colors, cut into 6" x 8" pieces, or 5" x 8" unlined index cards
- fine-line and broad-line felt-tipped markers in assorted colors
- fine-line black felt-tipped markers
- rulers
- hand mirrors

Doing the Project

1. Ask students to bring in their favorite trading cards (sports figures, personalities, game characters, etc.) on the day you introduce this project. It would also be helpful to have a few superhero comics on hand.

2. Distribute the "Superhero? That's Me" handout. Read through it with the students. Answer questions and provide explanations and details as needed. While students are working on their trading cards, be available to offer advice and assistance at each step.

3. Evaluate the students' projects, or have the students evaluate each other's projects. Which cards would they like to "collect"? Which cards do they think will be most valuable 10 years from now?

EXPERIENCE NOTES

The most difficult part of this project is usually the self-portrait. Have plenty of hand mirrors available. Encourage cartoon-style drawing, reassuring students that they only need to create an *impression*, not an exact likeness. Showing caricatures can help. Editorial cartoons are an excellent resource.

This project gives students an opportunity to affirm themselves—their physical features, abilities, special talents, and more.

Expanding on the Project

▪ Make photocopies of "The Real Me" cards and encourage trading among students. Lay out the student cards on legal-size paper (as many as possible per sheet), then copy the whole page and cut apart the cards. This is a wonderful self-esteem booster. Encourage the students to autograph their cards now, *before* they become famous!

▪ This project can be used as a book report technique for biographies. Students can make large hero/heroine cards that give details about the biography subjects in "trading card" fashion.

Alternative Projects

▪ Have students create "now and then" résumés. Show examples of résumés and brainstorm the kinds of information the students' résumés might include.

▪ Students can create their "Real Me" cards using photographs instead of drawings, and their "Fantastic Me" cards using illustrations cut from magazines.

Resources

Best-Maugard, Adolfo. *A Method for Creative Design.* (New York: Dover Publications, Inc., 1990.) Great help for borders; an excellent book for teaching basic design.

Superhero

That's Me!

Your fans are demanding trading cards about you! Since you are the expert on that subject, it's up to you to design and create your own cards.

You will make two cards: "The Real Me" and "The Fantastic Me." For "The Real Me," try to be objective about who you are and what you are interested in. For "The Fantastic Me," free your imagination and become the you of the future, or . . . ?

Card #1: The Real Me

The Front

1 Draw a self-portrait as you really are. This can be a close-up of your face or a full-length portrait. Leave 1/2" all around for a border.

2 Design your border. Try to relate it to one or more of your personal characteristics, talents, abilities, preferences, etc. You might draw a pattern that includes your favorite symbols, doodles, or colors.

3 Give your card a title or name.

4 Sign your autograph somewhere on the card.

The Back

1 List as many of your physical attributes as you want to include (height, weight, eye color, hair color, clothing sizes, etc.)

2 List the groups you belong to.

3 List your abilities, hobbies, interests, and anything you are famous for.

4 List your beliefs, likes, and dislikes.

5 Write a few lines about your history, birthplace, where you live now, siblings, parents, school, friends, etc.

6 Design a "crest" or symbol that represents you.

If you can't fit all six categories on the back of your card, choose the ones you most want to include.

Card #2: The Fantastic Me

Follow the same general guidelines as for Card #1, but this time, represent the "you" you might want to be (or could be) if anything was possible. Let your imagination soar! Become a superhero! Anticipate the future you! Be creative . . . be crazy . . . be inventive . . . elaborate.

Extra! Extra!

Thousands of newspapers, magazines, and tabloids are printed daily, each seeking to attract readers. The list of special-interest periodicals and publications seems endless. But is there such a thing as a "perfect" publication, just right for the individual reader? This project gives students the opportunity to create newspapers that reflect who they are.

Role Performance

Students create a personal newspaper.

Related Curriculum

Language Arts, Computer Skills, Math

Learning Objectives

By the end of this project, students will be able to:

* inventory their personal traits
* identify the parts of a newspaper
* complete several short articles and a layout
* exhibit improved computer and/or typing skills

Learning Styles

Affective, Cognitive, Individual

Materials Needed

* copies of the "Extra! Extra! Read All about Me" handout (pages 103–104) for each student
* an assortment of newspapers (dailies, tabloids, weekend editions) to use as samples, collected over a period of several weeks
* word processor(s), computer(s), or typewriter(s)
* plenty of paper, including 11" x 17" sheets for layout
* scissors
* rubber cement
* rulers
* colored pencils and markers
* stencils for hand lettering
* simple desktop publishing software (optional but recommended)

Doing the Project

1. Introduce the project by giving students time to look through the sample newspapers you have collected. Invite them to study and compare the different papers. Point out the various sections and explain the functions of each. If you need help, consult a journalism textbook.

2. Use questions like the following to begin a discussion, or have students write responses in their journals.

   ▶ Why would someone buy a newspaper?

   ▶ What is your favorite part of the newspaper? Why?

   ▶ What parts do you never read?

   ▶ Why would someone want to write for a newspaper?

   ▶ In your opinion, what are the best and worst parts of the paper? The most important parts?

   ▶ What do you think makes one paper different from another?

   ▶ If you were a section of the newspaper, what would you be? The headline? A feature article? The comics? Strictly sports? Good news? Disasters? The entertainment section? An editorial? Local news? The gossip column? The fashion page? The food column? The advice column?

   ▶ What other sections or categories might reflect who you are?

3. Distribute the "Extra! Extra! Read All about Me" handout. Read through it with the students. Answer questions and provide explanations and details as needed. While students are working on their newspapers, be available to offer advice and assistance at each step. They may need extra help determining "column inches" and finalizing page layouts. Remind them to be aware of margins and to use a ruler to line up their articles.

4. Evaluate the students' projects. Look for creativity, originality, and variety. How many different types of articles and features did the student include? How individualized are the final products? Consider the masthead, headlines, layout, and margins. You may want to create "award certificates" honoring each student for some aspect of his or her newspaper—Best Design, Best Reporting, Best Advice Column, etc. Afterward, set up a class "news stand" to display the students' papers.

EXPERIENCE NOTES

Even reluctant writers get absorbed in the possibilities of this project, so expect much creativity and enthusiasm. Students especially enjoy the trial-and-error process of laying out their newspapers, approaching the task as if it were a puzzle and delighting in "solving" it. If you have the resources, offer to make copies of the students' papers so they can read each other's news. Note that dark photographs will not copy well and should not be used if other options are available.

Awards are always a good idea. For a movie production project, I handed out "Zackademy Awards" on Oscars day. My students loved them!

Expanding on the Project

* Invite an expert to visit your class. This might be an editor or writer from a local newspaper, a journalism teacher, or the editor of a high school newspaper.

* Take a field trip to the offices of a city or neighborhood newspaper.

* Take a class survey to determine the students' special interests. Based on the survey results, form special interest small groups. Have each group create one or more newspapers on their interest to share with the class.

Alternative Projects

* Students with access to computers and modems could create "electronic newspapers" to post on local bulletin boards.

* Encourage strong writers to submit articles to local newspapers or national magazines that accept student submissions.

Resources

City newspapers often have free or low-cost classroom materials available for teaching students about the various parts of the newspaper. Check with your city newspaper.

Two excellent general resources for beginning journalists are:

—English, Earl, Clarence Hach, and Tom Rolnicke. *Scholastic Journalism*, 8th edition. (Ames, IA: Iowa State University Press, 1990.)

—Smith, Helen, editor. *Springboard to Journalism*, 5th edition. (New York: Columbia Scholastic Press Advisers Association of Columbia University, 1991.)

Microsoft's "Creative Writer" software, available in both Macintosh and Windows versions, has a very good newspaper format. Call Microsoft at 1-800-426-9400 to locate a retailer in your area who carries this program.

Henderson, Kathy. *Market Guide for Young Writers*, 4th edition. (Cincinnati, OH: Writer's Digest Books, 1993.) An authoritative, fact-filled "how-to-get-published" guide.

Whitfield, Jamie. *Getting Kids Published: A Practical Guide for Helping Young Authors See Their Works in Print*. (Waco, TX: Prufrock Press, 1994.)

Extra! Extra!

Read All about Me

Have you ever looked through an entire newspaper, only to find that a very few articles were interesting to you? Here's your chance to produce a newspaper with "all the news that's fit to print" . . . because it's all about YOU!

1 Consider the many different sections that appear in most newspapers. Brainstorm a list of sections you think you would like to include in your newspaper. Which sections are relevant to your personality, interests, abilities, and talents? Which have meaning to you and your life?

2 Read your brainstormed list and circle the sections you *will* include in your newspaper. Choose carefully. For example, if you love sports and participate in everything, then your sports section should be lengthy and comprehensive. However, if walking to the kitchen or running to the phone is your main exercise, then sports could be left out or handled humorously.

3 Design a distinctive banner and masthead for your newspaper. Include the name of your paper, the date of publication, the publisher, and the price per issue. You can do this by hand or use a computer with special fonts.

EXTRA! EXTRA!

4 Write your articles, features, ads, etc. Each one should reveal or reflect something about *you*. Suggestions:

- *Front page news:* A major event in your life (an honor or award, accomplishment, birthday, discovery, insight, etc.)
- *Travel section:* A vacation, visit to a relative, or "dream vacation"
- *Gossip column:* Amusing tips and facts about your friends and family (no rumors!)
- *Food section:* Your personal favorites, perhaps including recipes; grocery store ads
- *Arts & Entertainment section:* Reviews of your favorite movies, TV shows, and books; suggestions for things to do around your neighborhood, town, or city
- *Comics:* A single-frame cartoon or strip about a humorous event or incident in your life
- *Advice column:* If your friends often ask you for advice, this column should be easy to write
- *Letters to the editor (you):* Include "fan mail"
- *Sports section:* Your favorite sports; your latest achievements
- *Gripes and complaints column:* Things that bug you personally
- *Weather report:* If the weather means something to you personally; for example, "Rain forecast, weekend lawn mowing canceled"
- *Health section:* Describe things you do to stay healthy (your personal exercise program, healthful eating tips, stress-relieving strategies that work for you)
- *Family section*: Milestones in your family life and history
- *Horoscopes column:* Advice you'd like to give yourself; predictions of how your day (week, month) might go

5 Produce your newspaper. You might type your articles in columns, then lay them out on larger paper (cutting and pasting), or do everything (including the final layout) on a computer. **Boldface your titles** and make them larger than the text.

Add illustrations, photos, and cartoons. Make photocopies to paste on your final product. Or, if you have access to a scanner, scan your graphics into the computer and drop them into your layout.

If you're doing your layout on paper, *wait* to glue everything down until you're completely satisfied with the balance, variety, and composition. Remember that "less is more" when using rubber cement or glue on paper.

I'M A WORK OF ART

Is it possible to "get lost in a painting"? Absolutely! This activity takes students beyond the experience of becoming absorbed in a painting because of its beauty or mystery. Using their own creative ideas, they transform a painting they like and actually put themselves into it!

Role Performance

Students "re-create" a famous painting.

Related Curriculum

Art History

Learning Objectives

By the end of this project, students will be able to:

* survey famous paintings in any genre
* select a favorite artist
* modify a painting to include themselves
* think flexibly

Learning Styles

Affective, Cognitive, Individual

Materials Needed

* copies of the "I'm A Work of Art: Picture Me in a Painting" handout (pages 108–109) for each student
* a large assortment of visuals: books and catalogs containing reproductions of famous paintings, including paintings by modern artists; posters, slides, and postcards of famous paintings; old art magazines
* white construction paper
* rubber cement, white glue
* scissors
* fine-line felt-tipped colored markers
* paints and brushes
* overhead projector and/or slide projector
* blank acetates (for overheads) and overhead markers

Doing the Project

1. Introduce this project by showing a large quantity of art visuals. Pass around books, magazines, prints, and postcards; show overheads and slides; hang posters around the classroom. Invite the students to explore the visuals without giving specific instructions. The purpose of this introduction is exposure and pure enjoyment.

   If you use visuals from old calendars, magazines, etc., cut and separate the pictures before showing them to the students. Be sure to write the artist's name and the title of the work on the back of each one. You may want to laminate especially good pictures.

2. Distribute the "I'm a Work of Art: Picture Me in a Painting" handout. Read through it with the students. Answer questions and provide explanations and details as needed. While students are working on their personalized paintings, be available to offer advice and assistance at each step.

   Students may need special help deciding which painting to choose for their re-creation. Listen as they present their ideas about including themselves in the painting. Encourage them to "see" more than one possibility.

3. Evaluate the students' finished projects, or have the students evaluate each other's projects. (They love to discover each other "hiding" in the re-creations.) Afterward, arrange a clothesline display of the finished works. Play classical music during a "juice and cheese" reception for the artists. This would be an ideal Parents' Night activity.

EXPERIENCE NOTES

I like to begin this project by showing a large selection of art museum slides in a darkened room with light jazz music playing in the background. This sets the mood and allows the students to experience the art on a sensory level, without a lot of "teacher talk."

Expanding on the Project

- Ideally, this project will follow a field trip to an art museum or gallery. If this is not possible, ask local museums if they offer "outreach" programs, where speakers with slides visit classrooms. College art departments and local artists may be willing to help as well. If you have access to a computer with a CD-ROM, you can "tour" museums on the computer.

- Check your local library and video rental store for films of visits to famous museums and biographies of artists featuring examples of their art.

- Read aloud Chapter 2, "The Day Out," from *Mary Poppins* by P.L. Travers. In this chapter, Mary steps into a sidewalk chalk painting and becomes part of the painting.

Alternative Projects

- This project can be done with small groups as well. Have each group select a painting that will accommodate several inserted pictures or self-portraits.

- Have students (individuals or small groups) combine several parts of different paintings to create a new, "blended" masterpiece. It will take some very creative thinking to come up with a good title for this unique and original work of art.

Resources

Where can you get free art visuals? There are many possibilities, including:

— Ask staff members in museums and art galleries to save promotional posters for you to use. They receive them from other museums around the country and rarely hang them. Ask for damaged posters, postcards, or books as well. (Most museums and galleries are happy to help educate their future patrons.)

— Many libraries have excellent selections of art survey books with good reproductions. Also be sure to ask librarians for old catalogs and magazines that are due to be discarded.

— Used books stores often have an abundance of old art magazines.

— Art calendars are popular gifts that are often found abandoned in closets at the end of the year, so ask parents and other teachers for these valuable art resources.

Janson, H.W., and Anthony F. Janson. *The History of Art for Young People*, 4th edition. (New York: Harry N. Abrams, Inc., 1992.) If your school library doesn't have this book, ask them to buy it!

Lipman, Jean, and Richard Marshall. *Art about Art.* (New York: E.P. Dutton, Whitney Museum of Art, 1978.) This book is a catalog from an exhibit of artworks that paraphrased, re-created, or featured the work of old and modern masters in the art world. The examples show great creativity and humor.

Martin, Mary. *Start Exploring Masterpieces: A Fact-Filled Coloring Book.* (Philadelphia: Running Press Book Publishers, 1990.)

Massey, Sue. *Learning to Look: A Complete Art History & Appreciation Program for Grades K–8.* (Upper Saddle River, NJ: Prentice Hall, 1991.)

Taylor, Joshua. *Learning to Look: A Handbook for the Visual Arts.* (Chicago: University of Chicago Press, 1981.)

Travers, P.L. *Mary Poppins.* (New York: Dell Publishing, 1991.)

The Museum of Modern Art, 11 West 53rd Street, New York, NY 10019; telephone (212) 708-9400. Mail order department (for books, slides, and posters): (212) 708-9888.

I'm a Work of Art

Picture Me in a Painting

In the movie, *Mary Poppins*, there is a famous scene in which Mary "steps into" a sidewalk painting. She instantly becomes a part of the painting and changes it forever. You're about to put *yourself* into a great work of art—and change your view of it forever.

1 Look through art slides, museum exhibit catalogs, art magazines, books about various artists, posters, prints, art calendars, postcards, film strips, videos, etc. for examples of well-known paintings. Don't limit yourself to paintings of people. Look at all kinds—landscapes, still-lifes, abstractions, city scenes, etc.

2 Select an artist who "speaks" to you. Choose one work of art by that artist—something you'd like to become a part of. Study it carefully as you ask yourself these questions:

- Why did I choose this particular piece? What does it "say" to me?
- Why do I belong in this work of art?
- How can I become part of it?
- Where will I fit in?
- In what ways might I include myself in the painting?
- Will I represent myself abstractly or realistically?

Jot down answers on a separate sheet of paper or in your journal.

3 Decide how you will put yourself into the painting.

- Will you be the main subject or part of the background?
- If the reproduction is yours to keep, you many want to work directly on it, adding paint, drawings, photographs, or cutouts.
- If the reproduction is not yours to keep, photocopy it or create your own version, then add yourself.
- Whether you work with a print or a photocopy, "re-create" the work in whatever way(s) you choose. Change the colors, change the media, update the clothes, alter the size (enlarge it, reduce it, trim the edges, etc.).
- Try this easy transfer method, which uses a slide projector or overhead projector: Project a slide of your favorite painting (or a drawing of it on blank acetate) onto a large piece of white paper. Draw the projected lines to create a framework. Project a photograph (or drawing) of yourself onto the paper, superimposing your image over the painting or drawing. Experiment with different positions. When you see one you like, draw those lines onto the same paper.

4 Give your masterpiece a title. Sign your name. Be sure to give credit to the original artist in some way.

SELF QUILT

Texture, pattern, color, and design are all part of our physical environment, but nature makes it look easy! We humans, however, have many choices to make when creating our personal environment. This project gives students the experience of selecting textures, patterns, colors, and designs that reflect their personalities and combining them in a statement about themselves.

Role Performance

Students create a fabric quilt or collage.

Related Curriculum

Language Arts, Art, Home Economics

Learning Objectives

By the end of this project, students will be able to:
- think abstractly
- catalog their personal characteristics
- create a design out of fabric scraps
- exhibit improved crafts skills
- make an oral presentation

Learning Styles

Affective, Individual

Materials Needed

- copies of the "Self Quilt: Feeling Special" handout (pages 113–114) for each student
- large pieces of muslin or plain bed sheets
- a generous assortment of fabric scraps
- laundry baskets for sorting scraps
- cotton batting and/or fiberfill
- sewing needles and assorted threads
- hot glue gun, glue sticks, and/or white fabric glue
- assorted "stuff" to use as decorations—sequins, glitter, sandpaper, lace, leather, fake fur, buttons, twigs, bark, small plastics, fancy paper scraps, various trims, etc.
- permanent markers
- acrylic paints, paint brushes
- large resealable plastic bags for storing works in progress
- a sewing machine and an iron (both optional but helpful)

Doing the Project

1. Several weeks before beginning this project, start collecting fabric scraps. Sort them according to size, type, and color. Store them in several containers, such as laundry baskets, for easy access.

2. Introduce the project by giving each student a scrap of fabric chosen at random. Ask them to examine their scrap and fully describe its texture, appearance, color, weight, size, flexibility, etc. Ask them to name something that the fabric reminds them of—an object, a memory, a person, a concept, etc. Discuss how texture and color can create a mood or connotation in fabric as paint does on canvas. Use costume design and interior design as examples.

3. Distribute the "Self Quilt: Feeling Special" handout. Read through it with the students. Answer questions and provide explanations and details as needed. While students are working on their quilts, be available to offer advice and assistance at each step.

4. Evaluate the students' projects, emphasizing neatness and individuality. The quilts should be finished with sewn or glued edges and look complete.

EXPERIENCE NOTES

The resulting projects will vary greatly, according to each student's interest and ability levels. Encourage students to create patchwork wall hangings, pillows, place mats, or (for the truly ambitious) actual quilt coverings. Some will make simple squares or rectangles; others will come up with elaborate freeform designs with attachments, openings, and closures! Make it clear from the beginning that no sewing skills are required; the scraps can be glued onto a base fabric. Allow at least 3–4 class periods for this project. Play a little music while the students are working. This should be an enjoyable and relaxed activity, with much sharing and quiet conversation.

Expanding on the Project

- Check with local fabric stores for names of quilters who might be willing to visit your class as guest speakers. Quilting is a popular art form, with today's artists working with modern designs as well as traditional ones.

- Have small groups research the history of the American quilt and report back to the class. They might look into traditional patterns, styles, and designs, quilting bees as social gatherings, patchwork quilts, Amish quilts, African-American quilts, quilts in museum collections (including the Smithsonian), or other aspects of this fascinating art form.

Alternative Projects

- This project can be done with all recyclable materials, objects from nature, or different kinds of papers. (You or your students may decide not to use fabrics at all.)
- The "self quilt" concept also works well as photomontage. Have students tear pictures of textures from old magazines that have many color photographs and advertisements, then combine them in interesting ways.

Resources

It's really very easy to collect a wide variety of fabrics and scraps for this project, if you plan ahead and allow enough time. Suggestions:

—Ask fabric stores and drapery stores for sample pieces or remnants.

—Ask dressmakers and home economics teachers to save everything.

—If there are clothing manufacturers near you, ask for donations.

—Interior designers or building supplies stores may give you books of discontinued sample fabrics.

—Put a note in the PTA newsletter describing your project and asking for donations.

Many books are available on quilting and fiber art, and most libraries offer a good selection. One suggestion:

—Geis, Darlene. *The Quilt Encyclopedia Illustrated*. (New York: Harry N. Abrams, Inc., 1991.)

Write to craft museums for photos, slides, or pamphlets and postcards of quilted artworks or fabric collages. One suggestion:

—American Craft Museum, 40 W. 53rd St., New York, NY 10019; telephone (212) 956-6047.

SELF QUILT
Feeling Special

1 Think about the many times each day you touch some kind of fabric. On a separate sheet of paper, quickly brainstorm a list of the fabrics you come in contact with during a typical day.

2 Using fabrics and other materials as metaphors, try some abstract thinking about who you are. What textures, patterns, and colors represent your many aspects? Begin by considering these questions:

- Are you soft and light (silk, chiffon)?
- Rough and tough (leather)?
- Smooth (satin, plastic)?
- Do you often feel fuzzy (fake fur) or well-defined (vinyl)?
- Which are you most like: a busy pattern or a plain solid?
- Which describes you best: stripes or plaids?
- Are you basic and practical (cotton) or extravagant and expensive (silk, brocade, velvet)?

Add your own metaphors to this list.

SELF QUILT

3 Make a list of 10–12 of your personal characteristics. Match each one with a texture or fabric. (Keep thinking in metaphors!) Examples:

clean and neat = starched white cotton
dependable = blue denim
flexible thinker = spandex

4 Follow these steps to create a quilt or fabric collage that will communicate who you are. Each fabric, each decoration you choose should say something about you.

- Begin with a piece of plain fabric—any shape you choose, but no smaller than 10" x 12". This could be muslin or a piece of bed linen. If you want it to serve as a decorative backing, selection counts.

- Fold the edges and sew or glue them to prevent unraveling . . . unless you're feeling "frayed around the edges" and want that look.

- For an authentic quilted appearance, you might stitch or glue your backing to cotton batting or fiberfill.

- Select pieces of fabric from the class supply or bring your own.

- Arrange your fabric pieces on your backing in a pleasing, balanced design of your own creation. Play with the design until you're satisfied with it before stitching or gluing the pieces in place.

- Attach the pieces neatly and carefully. Remember that you are making a personal statement with your quilt.

- Express your individuality and creativity with elaboration and unusual materials, even things from nature, if appropriate.

- You may want to add fabric loops for display purposes. Hang your quilt from a painted dowel or a natural tree branch.

- Sign and date your finished work. Give it a title.

5 Present your quilt to the class, briefly explaining your choice of fabrics and composition and how the final product represents you.

Shoe Box Self

Everyone loves to collect things, and collections usually reflect something about the collectors—their preferences, interests, and personal style. This project challenges students to arrange a collection of "objects" that, when assembled, are representative of themselves.

Role Performance

Students assemble a collection of objects and create a box for display.

Related Curriculum

Language Arts, Math, Art

Learning Objectives

By the end of this project, students will be able to:

* create a list of personal characteristics, interests, ideals, beliefs, and details
* assemble a collection of various small objects and pictures that represent the self
* create a compartmentalized display box
* demonstrate improved crafts skills

Learning Styles

Affective, Individual

Materials Needed

* copies of the "Shoe Box Self: Crate Creations" handout (pages 118–119) for each student
* an assortment of boxes—boot boxes, hat boxes, wooden printer's trays, fruit or vegetable crates, etc.
* pieces of balsa wood, cardboard, foam core, wood scraps, etc. to use as shelves and partitions
* old magazines with photographs
* paper for sketching dimensions and ideas
* scissors
* hot glue gun, glue sticks, rubber cement
* hammer and small nails
* rulers
* paints (acrylics or spray enamels work best; temperas are too chalky and impermanent for this project)
* hooks and wires for hanging
* a variety of small personal objects (brought in by the students)

Doing the Project

1. Distribute the "Shoe Box Self: Crate Creations" handout. Read through it with the students. Answer questions and provide explanations and details as needed. While students are working on their boxes, be available to offer advice and assistance at each step.

   You may need to offer suggestions for objects and construction techniques. Encourage flexibility in designing the shape of the box. Skilled students may want to try boxes that are triangular, trapezoidal, or even columnar. Some may wish to hang appendages from the box or include electronics (lighting, sound, etc.).

   Remind them to be selective about the objects they choose to display. They should consider each one in terms of what it represents, its size, color, or shape, how it "fits" with the other objects, whether it adds to (or detracts from) the box design, and so on. Objects of great value or weight should not be included.

2. Evaluate the students' projects, or have students evaluate each other's projects. Look for originality, creativity, balance, variety in the selection of objects, and how accurately (and interestingly) the final box represents the individual. Afterward, you might arrange a "box museum" exhibit in the classroom and invite other classes to tour the exhibit.

It is very intriguing to watch students work on their boxes in class. The project is intensely personal, yet there tends to be a lot of conversation and sharing as students discuss construction techniques and ask each other, "What does *that* object mean?" Locating and choosing representing items becomes a treasure hunt for everyone. You will probably find yourself looking for objects, too.

There is a tendency for students to overdo it on this project—to make their boxes too complex or fill them with too many objects. Remind them of architect Mies Van der Rohe's famous quotation: "Less Is More."

Expanding on the Project

- Many modern artists have experimented with box collage construction, similar to this project. Introduce your students to the work of Joseph Cornell, who made intriguing assemblages in wooden boxes, and Louise Nevelson, who constructed enormous box sculptures from scrap wood, then painted them solid colors, creating a monumental impression.

Alternative Projects

* This project can be used to create a three-dimensional portrait of someone in history; to highlight a country; to commemorate an event; or to make a statement. The process is the same.

* Everyone needs a "treasure box"—a place to store letters, important "found" objects, and small, meaningful personal possessions. Collect a variety of small boxes with lids, or have students bring boxes from home. Have them decorate their boxes to reflect who they are. In other words, the *outside* will reveal something about themselves, but the objects *inside* will be secret.

Resources

The produce manager at your local grocery store may be an excellent source of fruit and vegetable boxes, which are perfect for this project. Produce managers throw these away daily, and they are usually happy to give them to teachers (instead of landfills).

McConnell, Gerald. *Assemblage: Three Dimensional Picture Making* (New York: Madison Square Press, 1976.)

Time Magazine, August 18, 1980. If you can borrow a copy of this magazine from your local library, the cover illustration—a box portrait of former President Jimmy Carter—features an excellent example of this type of art.

The Museum of Modern Art, 11 West 53rd Street, New York, NY 10019; telephone (212) 708-9400. Mail order department (for books, slides, and posters): (212) 708-9888.

SHOE BOX SELF

Crate Creations

Imagine that you live in a dormitory that requires an "identity box" to be attached to each resident's door. This box pictorially and abstractly represents the person who lives in that room. Others can look at the box and learn clues about him or her.

What pictures or objects will you put in your box? How will you represent yourself? What are you willing to reveal to the world? Is there anything you want to hide?

For this project, you will create a compartmentalized box of your own design. Inside your "identity box," you will place small objects and photographs that represent you and all that you are.

1 On a separate sheet of paper, brainstorm a list of your personal characteristics, interests, ideals, beliefs, details, etc. Make your list long to allow room for selectivity. Try for at least 25 items. Leave writing space beside each item on your list.

Shoe Box Self

2 Review your list and think carefully about each item. How would you represent it with something small and tangible? Try to come up with 1–2 ideas for each item on your list. Examples:

> I'm a runner = shoelaces
> I love the beach = a small shell and some sand
> I'm a musician = a 2" painted clay quarter note; a scrap of sheet music
> I'm emotional = a close-up photo of an eye with tears

3 Select a suitable box and put your name on the back. Measure the height, width, and depth, and record these measurements on paper. Start thinking about how you will divide your box into sections for display of your items. Consider including shapes other than the usual squares and rectangles. What about cylinders? (Cut cardboard tubes.) Or triangles? (Place slats at an angle.)

Sketch your ideas on paper before you begin construction. Gather the materials you need, cut them to shape, then use hot glue or small nails to secure your shelves, partitions, and spaces.

4 When the spaces within your box have been defined, paint your box. Paint the exterior and the back as well. Then add any finishing decorations and details.

Suggestion: Create at least one "hidden" compartment by attaching a little door or window. Store something "secret" inside.

5 Arrange your chosen objects inside your box. Move things around until you find the balance and look you want. Stand back, evaluate the effect, and make any last-minute changes before gluing your objects permanently in place.

Suggestion: Back a photograph with thin cardboard, cut out the main subject, and attach it to your box "freestanding." Or mount it to a small piece of foam board or sponge for a 3-D effect.

6 Finish your box by checking to see that all items are securely attached. Attach hooks or a wire if you plan to hang your box on a wall. Or let it stand as a table sculpture.

7 Sign and date your box. Give it a title.

Commemorative Stamp

Although the U.S. Post Office does not issue commemorative stamps for living persons, let's suppose they change the rules. This activity allows students to imagine and create a postage stamp bearing their own image.

Role Performance

Students draw a design for a stamp.

Related Curriculum

Language Arts, Art, Social Studies

Learning Objectives

By the end of this project, students will be able to:

- explore philately (the study of postage stamps)
- show improved symbolic thinking and elaboration skills
- create an intricate stamp design
- deliver a brief, persuasive speech

Learning Styles

Affective, Cognitive, Individual, Cooperative

Materials Needed

- copies of the "Commemorative Stamp: Picture This" handout (page 123) for each student
- white or manila paper, cut into 5" x 7" pieces
- colored pencils or fine-line felt-tipped markers
- stamp posters and information about current postal rates
- books about stamp collecting
- magnifying glasses
- assorted stamps (preferably a stamp collection)

Doing the Project

1. Divide the class into small groups. Give each group a selection of stamp posters, books about stamps and stamp collecting, a few stamps (if possible) and a magnifying glass, and other stamp-related materials you have gathered in advance. Instruct each group to look for, study, and discuss various aspects of stamps: themes, subjects, details, colors, composition, borders, monetary amounts, etc. Allow 15–20 minutes for this activity before calling the class back together.

2. Begin a discussion with questions like the following:

   ▶ What new and interesting things did you just learn about stamps?

   ▶ What surprised you? What would you like to know more about?

   ▶ Why do people collect stamps? (Ask if there are any stamp collectors in the room. Perhaps they would be willing to spend a few moments telling the class about their hobby.)

   ▶ Why do you think stamp collecting has international appeal?

   ▶ Why are so many different designs made for one monetary amount? Why not just make one design?

   ▶ What kinds of things could a person learn from collecting stamps?

   ▶ Do you ever notice the stamps on mail that comes to you or your family?

   ▶ What is the most interesting stamp you have ever seen?

   ▶ Of all the stamps you've seen, which one is your favorite?

   ▶ Why do you think people buy special stamps for invitations, holidays, and other occasions?

3. Distribute the "Commemorative Stamp: Picture This" handout. Read through it with the students. Answer questions and provide explanations and details as needed. While students are working on their stamp designs, be available to offer advice and assistance at each step. Shy students may need special help listing positive aspects about themselves.

   Some students may want to use a square shape or a larger rectangle than 5" x 7". Allow flexibility. Students who draw very simple designs may want to create a block of four designs that go together, as the postal system often does.

4. The oral presentation is a good opportunity for students to practice speaking persuasively and holding a visual while addressing an audience. This part of the project can be fun, but it can also be threatening for some, so encourage applause. Evaluate the students' projects based on creativity, imagination, how well a design represents the self, and the oral presentation. Afterward, display the students' stamps around the classroom.

EXPERIENCE NOTES

The best time to do this activity is before or after a new stamp is issued, which seems to happen frequently! This makes the topic "hot" and increases interest. Also, newspapers and magazines often run articles about stamps and collecting when important new stamps are issued—good background information for your students. (Remember all of the "Elvis stamp" attention?)

When my students do this project, I encourage them to submit their generic designs to the U.S. Postal Service Headquarters. (I haven't gotten a a response yet, but I keep trying!)

Expanding on the Project

※ This activity could be part of a unit on the U. S. Postal Service or a language arts unit on letter-writing.

※ Take a field trip to a local post office. (For main post offices in large cities, reservations are required. Even for smaller local post offices, they are recommended.) Have students prepare questions in advance about stamps, stamp collecting, and the U.S. postal system in general. Arrange to meet with an employee who is knowledgeable about stamp collecting. You may want to bring along a collection of your students' stamp designs and ask to have them displayed in the post office lobby.

※ Submit your students' stamp designs, ideas, suggestions, etc. to: Stamp Advisory U.S. Postal Service, Citizens' Stamp Advisory Committee, Room 5800, 475 L'Enfant Plaza, W. SW, Washington, D.C. 20260-6352. Or telephone the Main Post Office at (202) 268-2000 and ask them to direct your call.

※ Invite a guest speaker to your class who collects stamps, or have students bring in their own collections to share.

※ Encourage interested students to join the Junior Philatelists of America.

Alternative Projects

※ Have students create commemorative stamps for each other, their parents, best friends, teachers, the principal, etc. Or they might create commemorative stamps for a classroom event or special school project.

※ Have students create a series of stamps about themselves, perhaps in a block design. One stamp might show them as a child; another as a teenager; another as an adult who is famous for a particular accomplishment. This becomes an exercise in imagining their future selves.

Resources

The United States Post Office is your best resource for this project. Contact them in advance to request materials, catalogs, and information about current postal rates. Write on school letterhead stationery to: U.S. Postal Service, 475 L'Enfant Plaza, S.W., Washington, D.C. 20260-1540.

Your local post office may loan you a video about the postal service and give you old stamp posters, if notified in advance. You might also ask at your local post office how to obtain a copy of a booklet titled "The Wonderful World of Stamps," published by the U.S. Postal Service in 1987.

Best-Maugard, Adolfo. *A Method for Creative Design*. (New York: Dover Publications, Inc., 1990.) A classic book on the elements of design, with numerous drawings and ideas.

Lewis, Brenda Ralph. *Stamps! A Young Collector's Guide*. (New York: Dutton Children's Books, 1991.) An excellent guide to stamp collecting for young readers ages 8–14.

Junior Philatelists of America, P.O. Box 850, Boalsburg, PA 16827. An organization that helps young stamp collectors learn about the hobby. When requesting information, enclose a self-addressed, stamped #10 envelope.

The National Postal Museum, The Smithsonian Institution, Washington, D.C. 20560. Write for information and a request a copy of the *Art to Zoo Teacher's Guide*, *Magic in Your Mailbox: Learning from Letters and Other Mail*, September, 1993. Ask for a free teacher's subscription, too.

National First Day Cover Museum, 702 Randall Avenue, Cheyenne, WY 82001; (307) 771-3202. Displays first edition postage stamps, each bearing the date and postmark of the town where it was first issued. Write or call for information.

COMMEMORATIVE STAMP

Picture This

How would you like to be remembered 100 years from today? What qualities about you, achievements, or goals are important enough and special enough to be commemorated on a postage stamp? What do you expect to do in the future that will deserve to be recognized?

1 Brainstorm a list of ideas for a commemorative stamp about you. What are your interests? Abilities? Talents? Special qualities? Achievements? Future achievements?

2 What symbols could you use to represent your ideas? Draw a symbol or write a description next to each item on your brainstormed list. Your stamp might be a drawing of yourself, a drawing of yourself with symbols, or all symbols.

3 Decide on a monetary value for your stamp. Will it be a standard First Class stamp? Will it be an Air Mail stamp for use on mail you send to other countries? Will it be a post card stamp? (Check with your local post office to find out current monetary values for different types of stamps.)

4 Sketch a possible design for your stamp. Include all of the elements—your portrait, symbols, a border, the monetary value, and any other information you want to add. Pay close attention to composition and balance.

5 Draw your final design in pencil first, then use colored pencils or fine-line felt-tipped markers. The colors and lines should be clear and bright to simulate real stamp engravings.

6 To make your finished stamp look more realistic, cut a mock perforated edge around your stamp. (This effect can be created with a hand-held hole punch.)

7 Prepare a brief speech or oral presentation about your stamp. Your purpose will be to convince the "new stamp committee" (your classmates) that your stamp should be issued. You will need to explain why your stamp is important, inspiring . . . and potentially profitable for the postal system.

Where Do I Fit In?

This project is an exercise in abstract thinking and visual comprehension. Students place themselves in non-human situations and analyze choices. The results give you a greater understanding of each individual student's self-concept.

Role Performance

Students personify drawings.

Related Curriculum

Language Arts

Learning Objectives

By the end of this project, students will be able to:

- stretch the imagination
- reveal feelings
- apply personification to the self
- exhibit enhanced listening and analysis skills

Learning Styles

Affective, Cognitive, Individual

Materials Needed

- copies of the "Where Do I Fit In?" handout (pages 126–129) for each student
- colored pencils or fine-line felt-tipped colored markers

Doing the Project

1. Introduce the project with an imagination exercise. Have the students sit comfortably, close their eyes, relax, and breathe deeply as you read the following. Pause between sentences and paragraphs.

   "Imagine that you can change your form at will. You can become non-human. You can easily change your shape, but not your personality or the way you interact with others or with life in general.

   "Picture a bird flying on a cool, bright day, slowly flapping and gliding on wings of delicate bone and feathers. You are that bird for this moment in time. You are still yourself, but in the form of a bird. What is that like? How does it feel?

   "You fly and fly and decide to examine a forest below, when suddenly you decide to change form again. This time you become a tree, with roots and branches and leaves. The location you select is important to you, so you stay there awhile, experiencing the sights, smells, and sounds of the forest.

"After a day or two, you get restless. You decide to follow the sounds on a road nearby. You become a car. What kind of car do you become? Your adventure takes you far and you enjoy the ride, but you end up in a traffic jam. You sit and contemplate where you fit in. You notice the other cars, and you feel different and unique. You know who you are.

"Hungry for another experience, you follow a group of people until they enter the door to a cafeteria. You change your form again and become something to eat or drink. You are now a food or a beverage. What are you? Someone reaches for you, puts you on a tray, and carries you to a table. You are still you—the true you."

Let the students enjoy this experience for a few minutes, then ask them to slowly open their eyes and take a deep breath. Some may giggle; some may want to talk about the experience. Welcome comments and questions.

2. Distribute the "Where Do I Fit In?" handout. Read through it with the students. Allow about seven minutes for students to complete each part—about half an hour for all four parts.

3. Follow up with a group discussion or individual conferences. If you choose a group discussion, invite the students to sit in a circle to share some of the feelings and insights they experienced while doing this project. (Some students will want to share; others may not.) You might prepare some sentence beginnings ahead of time for the students to complete while sitting in the circle. Examples:

▶ My tree was _____ because _____.

▶ If I was a car, I'd be a _____.

This project would be a good prompt for a "boundary breaking" session. However you decide to present it, no evaluation is necessary.

EXPERIENCE NOTES

You may want to let students take their handouts home and complete them at their own pace. Set a time limit—perhaps 1–2 days—when everyone must have their handouts done.

This project is a challenging stretch for the imagination, one that inspires students to use personification more in their personal writing. My students tend to make greater use of metaphors after completing this project. Some have told me that they can't see birds on power lines without thinking of this project and wondering about the "bird interactions."

Expanding on the Project

▪ Invite students to continue this activity, creating their own imaginary non-human situation(s) and placing themselves in the picture(s).

▪ You might use the handout as a way to analyze peer relationships. In private conferences with individual students, ask questions like, "Who do you think is the lonely tree in the forest? The bird in the corner?"

Alternative Projects

▪ Read and discuss stories that personify objects or animals, such as Richard Bach's *Jonathan Livingston Seagull* or Trina Paulus's *Hope for the Flowers*. The Paulus book is especially rich in meaningful themes: love, striving for something, leading and following, taking time to care and relate to others as you pursue a goal.

Resources

Bach, Richard. *Jonathan Livingston Seagull*, 20th Anniversary Edition. (New York: Macmillan Publishing Co., 1990.)

Paulus, Trina. *Hope for the Flowers*. (New York: Paulist Press, 1972.)

Where Do I Fit In?

Look briefly at the illustrations on pages 128–129, then come back and read the instructions on pages 126 and 127.

A. Birds on Wires

At certain times of the year, flocks of birds can be seen (and heard) congregating at city intersections on telephone and power lines. There seems to be a strong social order among them. As you look at the illustration, imagine that you are one of the birds in the flock. Look at the positions and interactions of the birds, then decide which bird you are. Circle that bird. In the space provided, explain why you relate to that particular bird.

B. In the Forest

In a natural forest, you will often see a variety of trees in many sizes and configurations. Some large trees stand alone; others have little trees growing beneath their branches. Sometimes you'll see a cluster of small trees in a separate space or a whole section of old, tall, skinny trees. Study the illustration of the forest and decide which tree you are. Circle the tree that represents you at this time in your life. Where do you stand in the forest? Are you alone, or are you near the others? What makes you different or the same? Elaborate and explain your answers in the space provided.

Where Do I Fit In?

C. Gridlock

"Gridlock" is a term for a traffic jam in which no vehicle can move in any direction. If you were a car in the gridlock shown in the illustration, what kind of car would you be? Sporty? Secure? Dependable? Where would you be in the illustration? Where do you usually find yourself in life? In the front, stuck in the middle, following others? Setting the pace? The fast lane? The slow? In the carpool? Alone? Unsure of your direction? Be a car and abstractly apply these questions to yourself. Color, decorate, or circle the car that is you. Use the space provided to explain your selection as it relates to you.

D. Cafeteria

We all need food to survive, yet we all relate to it differently. Some foods bring back memories; other foods are very important to some people, less important to others. Some people choose not to eat certain kinds of foods for religious, cultural, or personal reasons. Forget which foods you like or dislike. Imagine that you are a food (or a beverage). Which food are you and why? Are you the main course? A staple food (bread, rice, etc.)? An appetizer? A salad? Dessert? How do others see you in the "cafeteria of life"? Look at the different foods shown in the illustration. Decide which one best represents you. Circle it or color it in. Use the space provided to explain your choice.

A. Birds on Wires

B. In the Forest

C. Gridlock!

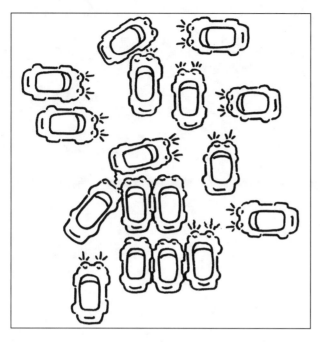

D. Cafeteria

INDEX

ABOUT THE AUTHOR

Linda R. Zack, M.Ed., has been a certified teacher of gifted children for more than 12 years. In 1994, she received the Amway/*Newsweek* "Class Act" award and was named AT&T's Environmental Teacher of the Year for Florida middle schools. Her students have won numerous awards in Odyssey of the Mind competitions, Junior Orange Bowl Parade float competitions, Knowledge Master Open competitions, and national writing contests. Linda teaches full-time at Arvida Middle School in Miami, Florida.

Photograph by Tracey Zack

MORE FREE SPIRIT BOOKS

Becoming Myself:
True Stories about
Learning from Life

by Cassandra Walker Simmons

A TV personality and popular speaker reveals the secrets of her success—self-esteem, strong values, and a supportive family—in dozens of true stories about growing up. Her personal experiences and practical advice inspire readers to believe in themselves and be the winners they are meant to be. Ages 11 and up.

$4.95; 144 pp.; s/c; 5 1/8" x 7 1/2"

The Best of Free Spirit®:
Five Years of Award-Winning
News & Views on Growing Up

by the Free Spirit Editors

Hundreds of articles, tips, and cartoons on topics including "Self-Awareness and Self-Esteem," "Making a Difference," "Diversity," "Family and Friends," "Study Skills and Test-Taking Tips," and more. Everything is reproducible for home and classroom use. Ages 10 and up.

$24.95; 256 pp.; illust.; s/c; 8 1/2" x 11"

Class Rules Poster

Ten time-tested "class rules" encourage kids to respect themselves and one another, take risks, ask questions, and stick up for themselves. Adapted from **Managing the Social and Emotional Needs of the Gifted.** For all ages.

$5.00; 17" x 22"

Doing the Days:
A Year's Worth of Creative
Journaling, Drawing, Listening,
Reading, Thinking, Arts & Crafts
Activities for Children Ages 8–12

by Lorraine M. Dahlstrom

1,464 fun learning activities linked to the calendar year span all areas of the curriculum and stress whole language, cooperative learning, and critical thinking skills. Grades 3–6.

$21.95; 240 pp.; illust.; s/c; 8 1/2" x 11"

The First Honest Book about Lies

by Jonni Kincher

Is it ever okay to lie? Are some lies worse than others? Experiments, examples, and games encourage readers to explore the nature of lies, become active questioners and truth-seekers, and explore their own feelings about lies. Ages 13 and up.

$12.95; 176 pp.; illust.; s/c; 8" x 10"

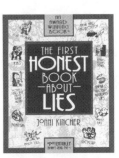

Girls and Young Women Inventing:
20 True Stories about Inventors
and Their Inventions

by Frances A. Karnes, Ph.D., and Suzanne M. Bean, Ph.D.

Not just for girls and young women, this book will inspire and motivate all young inventors. Includes real-life stories by successful young inventors, step-by-step instructions on how to be an inventor, up-to-date information about inventors' associations and organizations, a timeline of women inventors, quotations, and a comprehensive list of suggested readings. Ages 11 and up.

$12.95; 176 pp.; B&W photos; s/c; 6" x 9"

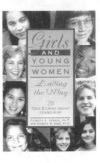

It's All In Your Head:
A Guide to Understanding
Your Brain and Boosting
Your Brain Power

by Susan L. Barrett

An "owner's manual" on the brain that kids can understand. Revised and updated edition includes new brain facts; new definitions of intelligence and creativity; new information on left- and right-brain function; new facts on how diet, exercise, and sleep affect the brain; and more. Ages 9–14.

$9.95; 160 pp.; illust.; s/c; 6" x 9"

Also available:

A Teacher's Guide to
It's All in Your Head

by Susan Barrett

$6.95; 52 pp.; s/c; 8 1/2" x 11"

The Kid's Guide to Service Projects:
Over 500 Service Ideas
for Young People Who
Want to Make a Difference
by Barbara A. Lewis

Projects range from simple things anyone can do to large-scale commitments that involve whole communities. Kids can choose from a variety of topics including animals, crime, the environment, literacy, politics, and more. "Service Project How-Tos" offer step-by-step instructions for creating fliers, petitions, and press releases, fundraising, and more. Ages 10 and up.

$10.95; 184 pp.; s/c; 6" x 9"

The Kid's Guide to Social Action:
How to Solve the Social Problems
You Choose—and Turn Creative
Thinking into Positive Action
by Barbara A. Lewis

This comprehensive guide to making a difference in the world teaches letter-writing, interviewing, speechmaking, fundraising, lobbying, getting media coverage, and more. Ages 10 and up.

$14.95; 208 pp.; illust.; B&W photos; s/c; 8 1/2" x 11"

Laughing Together:
Giggles and Grins from
Around the Globe
by Barbara K. Walker
illustrated by Simms Tabeck

Hundreds of jokes, riddles, rhymes, and short tales promote multiculturalism and global awareness through laughter, the universal language. Many are printed in their original language as well as English. For all ages.

$12.95; 128 pp.; illust.; s/c; 7 1/4" x 9 1/4"

Psychology for Kids:
40 Fun Tests That Help You
Learn About Yourself
by Jonni Kincher

Based on sound psychological concepts, this fascinating book promotes self-discovery, self-awareness, and self-esteem. It helps to answer questions like, "Are you an introvert or an extrovert?" and "What body language do you speak?" and empowers kids to make good choices about their lives. Ages 10 and up.

$14.95; 160 pp.; illust.; s/c; 8 1/2" x 11"

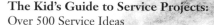

40 Fun Experiments That
Help You Learn About Others
by Jonni Kincher

Based on sound psychological concepts, these experiments explore thought-provoking questions like, "Are people more logical or more emotional?" and "Does competition improve performance?" In the process, readers sharpen their observation skills; gain experience collecting and evaluating data; and learn more about their family, friends, classmates, and themselves. Ages 12 and up.

$16.95; 168 pp.; illust.; s/c; 8 1/2" x 11"

Tips for Making and Keeping
Friends Poster

Stimulate and reinforce important social skills with this colorful poster. Adapted from **The Gifted Kids Survival Guide II**, it spells out ten essential tips for forming and strengthening friendships, from "be accepting" to "be honest." For the classroom, youth room, or home. For all ages.

$6.00; 17" x 22"

TNT Teaching:
Over 200 Dynamite Ways to
Make Your Classroom Come Alive
written and illustrated by Randy Moberg

Hundreds of fresh, exciting ways to present the curriculum, plus new uses for media equipment—even a course in cartooning. A wonderful resource for your Free Spirited Classroom. Grades K–8.

$19.95; 160 pp.; illust.; s/c; 8 1/2" x 11"

The Young Person's Guide to
Becoming a Writer
by Janet E. Grant

This comprehensive guide to starting and maintaining a writing career encourages young writers to discover their writing style, experiment with genres, evaluate their own work, and submit manuscripts for publication. Includes activities, tips, places to contact, recommended readings, and much more. Ages 12 and up.

$13.95; 176 pp.; s/c; 6" x 9"

Find these books in your favorite bookstore, or write or call:

Free Spirit Publishing Inc.
400 First Avenue North, Suite 616
Minneapolis, MN 55401-1730
Toll-free (800)735-7323, Local (612)338-2068
Fax (612) 337-5050